DATE DUE FOR RETURN

09. JUN 94		

The Public Papers of Chief Justice EARL WARREN

EDITED BY HENRY M. CHRISTMAN

GREENWOOD PRESS, PUBLISHERS
WESTPORT, CONNECTICUT

Library of Congress Cataloging in Publication Data

Warren, Earl, 1891-1974.
  The public papers of Chief Justice Earl Warren.

  Reprint of the 1959 ed.
  1. Judicial opinions--United States. 2. Cali-
fornia--Politics and government--Addresses, essays,
lectures.
[KF213.W34C53 1974]   347'.73'2634   74-10019
ISBN 0-8371-7654-9

The article "The Law and the Future" was published originally in the November 1955 issue of Fortune and is copyrighted © 1955 by Time Inc.

Originally published in 1959 by Simon and Schuster, New York

Reprinted with the permission of Henry M. Christman

Reprinted in 1974 by Greenwood Press,
a division of Williamhouse-Regency Inc.

Library of Congress Catalog Card Number 74-10019

ISBN 0-8371-7654-9

Printed in the United States of America

Contents

I

California and the Nation:

The Governor Speaks His Mind

CONSTITUTIONAL REFORM AND THE
DEVELOPMENT OF STATE GOVERN-
MENT
*Address to the Legislative Joint Interim
Committee on Constitutional Revision
Santa Barbara, California, October 29, 1947*

PAGE 3

EDUCATION
*Address to the National Convention of the
National Education Association
San Francisco, California, July 2, 1951*

PAGE 11

EQUAL RIGHTS FOR ALL
*Address to the National Convention of the
Anti-Defamation League of B'nai B'rith
Los Angeles, California, May 6, 1948*

PAGE 14

v

CONTENTS

PENAL REFORM
"California's Sentencing and Correctional
Methods," Address to the National Conven-
tion of the American Bar Association, Sec-
tion on Criminal Law
Atlantic City, New Jersey, October 29, 1946

PAGE 19

PUBLIC HEALTH
Address to the National Convention of the
American Public Health Association
San Francisco, California, October 30, 1951

PAGE 31

THE REPUBLICAN PARTY
Lincoln Day Address, Middlesex Club Lin-
coln Day Dinner
Boston, Massachusetts, February 12, 1952

PAGE 38

THE HOPES OF MAN
Address of Welcome to the Founding Dele-
gates of the United Nations
San Francisco, California, April 25, 1945

PAGE 47

Address Commemorating the Centennial of
the Discovery of Gold in California
Coloma, California, January 24, 1948

PAGE 49

vi

CONTENTS

Address of Welcome to the Delegates of the
Japanese Peace Treaty Conference
San Francisco, California, September 4, 1951

PAGE 53

II

Liberty and the Law:

Addresses of the Chief Justice

Address at the Eighty-sixth Charter Day Exercises of the University of California
Berkeley, California, March 23, 1954

PAGE 59

"The Blessings of Liberty," Address at the
Second Century Convocation of Washing-
ton University
St. Louis, Missouri, February 19, 1955

PAGE 66

Address at the Centennial Celebration for
Robert M. La Follette, Sr.
Madison, Wisconsin, June 10, 1955

PAGE 76

vii

CONTENTS

Response to an Address by the President of
the United States at the John Marshall Bicentennial Ceremonies of the American Bar
Association
Philadelphia, Pennsylvania, August 24, 1955

PAGE 84

Address at the Justice Louis Dembitz Bran-
deis Centennial Convocation of Brandeis
University
Waltham, Massachusetts,
November 11, 1956

PAGE 89

"A Way of Life," Address at the Veterans
Day Brotherhood Luncheon of the National
Conference of Christians and Jews
New York, November 12, 1956

PAGE 96

Response to an Address by the Rt. Hon.
Viscount Kilmuir, Lord High Chancellor of
Great Britain, at the American Bar Associ-
ation Convention in Westminster Hall
London, England, July 24, 1957

PAGE 102

III

The Scales of Justice:

Supreme Court Decisions

EQUALITY BEFORE THE LAW
Pete Hernandez v. State of Texas
347 US 475, 98 L ed 866, 74 S Ct 667
Decided May 3, 1954

PAGE 109

Oliver Brown et al. v. Board of Education of
Topeka
347 US 483, 98 L ed 873, 74 S Ct 686
Decided May 17, 1954

PAGE 114

Spottswood Thomas Bolling et al. v. C. Melvin Sharpe et al.
347 US 497, 98 L ed 884, 74 S Ct 693
Decided May 17, 1954

PAGE 123

Oliver Brown et al. v. Board of Education of
Topeka
349 US 294, 99 L ed 1083, 75 S Ct 753
Decided May 31, 1955

PAGE 125

CONTENTS

JUSTICE UNDER LAW
Commonwealth of Pennsylvania v. Steve Nelson
350 US 497, 100 L ed 640, 76 S Ct 477
Decided May 14, 1956

PAGE 130

Stephen Mesarosh, also known as Steve Nelson, et al. v. United States of America
352 US 1, 1 L ed 2d 1, 77 S Ct 1
Decided November 5, 1956

PAGE 140

John T. Watkins v. United States of America
354 US 178, 1 L ed 2d 1273, 77 S Ct 1173
Decided June 17, 1957

PAGE 150

Paul M. Sweezy v. State of New Hampshire
354 US 234, 1 L ed 2d 1311, 77 S Ct 1203
Decided June 17, 1957

PAGE 175

Albert L. Trop v. John Foster Dulles, Secretary of State of the United States of America
356 US 86, 2 L ed 2d 630, 78 S Ct 590
Decided March 31, 1958

PAGE 191

THE CHIEF JUSTICE DISSENTS
Cecil Reginald Jay v. John P. Boyd, District Director, Immigration and Naturalization Service
351 US 345, 100 L ed 1242, 76 S Ct 919
Decided June 11, 1956

PAGE 205

CONTENTS

Clemente Martinez Perez v. Herbert
Brownell, Jr., Attorney General of the
United States of America
356 US 44, 2 L ed 2d 603, 78 S Ct 568
                    Decided March 31, 1958

PAGE 207

IV

The Law and the Future:

The Chief Justice Looks Ahead

"The Law and the Future," an article by
Chief Justice Warren published in the November 1955 issue of Fortune magazine

PAGE 221

Editor's Note

EARL WARREN *needs no introduction. His achievements speak for themselves.*

A word about the preparation of this volume is in order. In the editor's judgment, it includes many of the most famous and significant papers from the many years the Chief Justice has devoted to public service. No book can be all-inclusive, however, and the editor regrets that various other documents, also of interest and significance, could not be published as well.

So that the compilation of papers might be as thorough as possible, the editor requested permission to consult the files of the Chief Justice. The Chief Justice kindly granted the request; and this was the extent of his participation in the book. The editor bears sole responsibility for the book, for the selections therein, and for the initiation of this publishing endeavor.

Two editorial features should be noted here. In their original form, the addresses in Section I contained miscellaneous details which had meaning only for the listening audience. These references have been omitted. In Section III, the original footnotes, which consisted primarily of case-number citations, have also been omitted. There is no other abridgment whatever.

No book can be published without the assistance of many persons; and to each and all of those who helped at one step or another with this volume, the editor extends grateful thanks.

HENRY M. CHRISTMAN

I

California and the Nation

The Governor
Speaks His Mind

Constitutional Reform

and the Development

of State Government

Address to the Legislative Joint Interim Committee on Constitutional Revision and its Advisory Committees

Santa Barbara, California
October 29, 1947

I AM VERY GLAD that I have been able to accept your kind invitation to be present as you undertake your work of constitutional revision.

As we look not only to the past but also to the future, we naturally consider the kind of state we would like our children and their children to live in during this next one hundred years. The constitution under which they are to live will determine very largely what kind of state it will be.

Ordinarily the writing of a new constitution or the general

revision of an old one would be done by delegates elected by the people for that specific purpose. There would be a constitutional convention, accompanied by public debate over the various issues involved.

I personally would have preferred such a procedure if it is the intention to thoroughly revise our constitution. I like to follow established constitutional procedures, particularly when they involve participation by the people through representatives elected for a specific purpose. It shares the responsibility for good government directly with the people. It shows a mutual relationship of trust and confidence that is essential to a democratic system. The more we in public office trust the people, the more the people will trust us.

The Legislature, however, also has the right under the constitution to submit amendments to the people for their approval; and if it decides to submit a new or revised constitution to the people through a series of amendments designed for the purpose, then it becomes the duty of all public officials to assist the Legislature in the drafting of such amendments as will provide the foundation for a sound and progressive government in the years that lie before us.

Nevertheless, the people having directed in 1934 that a constitutional convention be held, we should bear in mind that, when the mandate of the people is departed from, we assume an added responsibility to protect them at all costs from every influence that does not square with broad public interests. In no other way can the people be served.

I want to be helpful to you in accomplishing this result, and the facilities of my office are available to you at all times.

The story of constitutional development in California is well worth our attention.

During the thirty years between 1849, when our first constitution was adopted, and 1879, when our present constitution was adopted, California experienced for the most part a period of rollicking boom.

First, there were the gold mines and their feverish development; then the nearby silver discovery and its financial exploitation in our state; then the growth of agriculture and manufacturing to meet the needs of the growing communities; then the building of the railroad that in 1869 displaced the coaches and the pony express of the fifties and the sixties.

Population had been growing at an almost unbelievable rate. In 1848, when gold was discovered, there were, besides the Indians, only fifteen thousand people in the entire state. By 1850, there were, according to the Federal census, 92,000, and by 1880 the population had grown to 864,000. Nevertheless, during that period there seemed to be room and work and opportunity for everybody in California.

Absorbed in the quest for a share in the riches, the average Californian was too preoccupied to pay much attention to the condition of his state government. The constitution of 1849 seemed to be good enough. It was amended only three times in thirty years and several attempts to revise it by constitutional convention failed.

In the seventies, however, came a time of reckoning. The boom period had run its course. Banks failed, business bankruptcies flared, mining stocks collapsed. The farmers lost their markets and unemployment spread throughout the state.

Toward the end of the seventies the people of California, aroused by this state of affairs, turned their eyes for the first time upon their state government. What, they asked, had it been doing for their welfare and protection during these years of growth and activity? They found to their amazement that during this period of complacency their state government had become top-heavy with special interests, that it had fallen so completely under the domination of powerful groups that it had virtually ceased to represent the public interest.

The resentment of the people was prompt and strong. A demand arose for constitutional reform, and out of that demand came the present constitution of 1879.

The new constitution, although dimly reflecting the bitterness of the people at the time, accomplished substantial reforms. The public disillusionment of the time, however, was registered in its numerous provisions restricting the powers of the state government.

Another thirty-year period passed during which state government again succumbed to selfish domination—influences that paralyzed it to a degree that prevented proper response to the public need.

In 1911, another political revolution broke forth and fought its way with a series of constitutional amendments to the accomplishment of the initiative, the referendum and the recall, the strengthening of the Railroad Commission, and the establishment of a system of workmen's compensation.

Since that time another cycle of thirty-five years has passed and, although the people of this state have been preoccupied recently with depression, war, and postwar problems, there is still, in my opinion, an underlying insistence on their part that their government keep itself independent, alert to public need, and prepared to meet the requirements that are piling up for the future.

Whether state government in California will be able to keep faith with, and squarely meet, the expectation of our people, depends largely upon the content and the spirit of its constitution.

The resolution under which your committee is working points out that numerous amendments have encumbered, complicated and lengthened the present constitution and that there is, therefore, a need for corrective amendment, revision and simplification.

This suggests one of the approaches to constitutional revision—the revision of the *form* of the document.

It is true that the present constitution has been frequently criticized for its size—72,000 words, in contrast to the 7,500 words of the Federal Constitution. It has also been criticized because of its encumbering amendments—256 in all since 1879. There is, therefore, need for a revision that will make the document more a statement of principles than a collection of specific statutory provisions.

I think we can all agree that the ideal would be to make our constitution so compact and so simple that it would be quite understandable to our young people as they reach the age of citizenship. It is well to remember, however, that any attempt to revise a document which records the struggle of the people to establish and preserve their basic rights involves a serious responsibility.

Whether a constitution be long or short, clumsy or streamlined, and whether its amendments have been few or many, it is, nevertheless, a solemn expression from the people of their understanding with their government. It is the method by which the American people have sought to protect themselves against domination by the state, or domination of the state by any group whose interests are less extensive than the people as a whole.

I believe, therefore, that it would be a mistake to make a fetish of mere size or form or simplification at the expense of positive provisions for the protection of the public interest —the paramount objective of any constitution. That would be sacrificing substance for form.

The heart of any constitution consists of its bill of rights, those provisions that secure to the people their liberty of

7

conscience, of speech, of the press, of lawful assembly, and the right to uniform application of the laws and to due process of law.

Every other provision of the constitution should be designed in the spirit of these basic rights in order to make sure that they become not mere theoretical rights, but actual rights that can be translated by our people into practical opportunities for self-development in their homes, at their work, and even during their leisure hours.

To the constitution we look for the preservation of those humane and progressive institutions for which people have struggled so hard and with respect to which California has frequently been a leader in the nation.

To the constitution we look for provisions that will guarantee an equitable system of taxation and the financial integrity of the state; for provisions that establish a civil service for the competent administration of public affairs; for a balance between the legislative, executive, and judicial branches of government, and such a clear statement of their respective jurisdictions that the people may be able to place responsibility.

To the constitution we also look for an election system that will keep the right of suffrage inviolate and effective, and for those protective procedures, such as the initiative, the referendum and the recall, that secure to the people the ultimate control of their framework of law and order.

To the constitution, likewise, we should be able to look for directives that will call for the careful conservation and wise use of those magnificent natural resources that have been given to us in trust to meet the human needs of the present and the future.

Upon all these subjects our approach to constitutional revision must be made with a view to the needs of people in a state that has grown twelvefold in population since their present constitution was adopted—a state that will continue to grow from its present ten million to twenty million, I am sure, within the next few decades.

This kind of growth has been in the past a constant and compelling pressure for the development of our natural resources, our enterprises and our public services. It is likewise the source from which we obtain the manpower and the markets that make this development possible.

Growth, therefore, brings to California its great opportunities, but at the same time it creates great problems— problems that become complex in proportion to size. These problems must be met squarely and constructively no matter how new or complex they may be.

There was never a time that called for greater alertness and ingenuity on our part to make democracy serve the public interest. Our form of government is today on trial. We are the object of propaganda designed to make it appear that democracy lacks character, lacks efficiency and a genuine desire to meet the needs of common men and women. Our only defense against this demagoguery is a renewal of our effort to make democratic government ever more responsive to the public need—not the needs of some, but the needs of all, the needs of ordinary people in their homes who must of necessity rely upon their elected representatives to watchfully protect their stake in government.

This is particularly true today with respect to state government. It is becoming more and more apparent that the solution of many problems that vex our people and block community progress should not be left for solution to an already overburdened national government—a national government that will be absorbed during these coming years with the wider problems of national security and world peace. State government must, therefore, stand as firmly as possible upon its own feet and draw fully upon all of its own resources.

Only in this way will we be able to meet our full responsibility and at the same time avoid centralized bureaucracy which in the abstract we deplore but which in our state and local governments we too often encourage by our own inaction.

It seems to me, therefore, that the time and place and purpose of your meeting combine to inspire all of us to great and unselfish public service. We who occupy public office are dealing with the rights, the welfare and the future of millions. Their government is for the time being entrusted to our hands.

This is a great responsibility—a responsibility involving great difficulties but, if well done, still greater satisfactions.

It is my firm belief that if we fully realize our responsibility and faithfully follow these principles, California will receive from your hands a constitutional document worthy of a great state—a constitution which our people can approve and upon which they and their children can safely rely in the years to come.

Education

Address to the National Convention of
the National Education Association

San Francisco, California, July 2, 1951

You ARE VERY WELCOME to our state. Certainly you know that to be true, because this is the eighth time you have so favored us. We feel honored that you would return so often to California for your assemblies.

We admire you for your insistence that all children everywhere, rich and poor and handicapped, have the same opportunity for a sound, basic education.

You come to us at an important time in the school history of our state. We are wrestling with problems of administration, of improving teacher training, raising qualifications and salaries, of maintaining academic freedom, of constructing schools, of increasing state aid per unit of attendance, and of establishing the principle of equalization for the poorer districts. We are working at these things co-operatively, recognizing the joint responsibility of state and community to provide adequate education for all our children

11

without regard to whether they live in a rich or a poor district. Education will never be sound until this principle of equalization is recognized and practiced, both in the states and nationally.

There are states in America today which because of rapidly mounting school enrollments, higher living costs and critical shortages of elementary teachers, do not and cannot, unless assisted by the Federal Government, maintain educational standards adequate to present-day needs.

A school child is not merely the responsibility of his school district, but he is also a citizen of the state, which properly maintains and controls the educational system. But more than that he is an American with a birthright. That birthright entitles him to be taught in the public school in his neighborhood the fundamentals of our civilization, the foundation for making an honorable living, the reciprocal privileges and responsibilities of American citizenship, the advantages of our way of life, the place of his country in the world at large, and his place in both.

There are those who contend that this is no time to be talking about advancing social objectives. They even suggest that it would be desirable to cut back on them. Nothing could be farther from reality.

A nation that abandons its social objectives is on the road to decadence. Within the limits of our financial means every social objective of the American people must be advanced not only to relieve undue hardship and afford equal opportunity for the good life, but also to demonstrate to an observing and critical world that our governmental and economic systems can work hand in hand in the elimination of poverty, suffering and degradation. And we must demonstrate also to the cynical part of the world that we can and will, as long as it may be necessary, defend ourselves against aggression on the part of any nation on earth.

The greatest of all our social objectives, of course, is to have an enlightened citizenry. The foundation for such a citizenry is to be found in universal public education. We must, therefore, strengthen our public school system, today, tomorrow, and every day, until it serves its true purpose everywhere.

You are charged with the responsibility of serving all our children with an educational plan suited to the range of capacity of the various elements in our population, from the lowest educable group to the genius, from the scholarly to those who are adapted to technical skills. We ask that our physically handicapped have the best possible education and be made self-supporting if possible. In short, we want every person trained so that he can have the greatest possible self-fulfillment.

In the doing of this job I know you are harassed on both sides—on the one hand by those who would resist all change even though we are living in a fast-changing world, on the other hand by those who are contemptuous of the past and would have you cut loose from your moorings and pursue some will-o'-the-wisp ideology just because it is different.

It is difficult to remain somewhere between these two, adhering to those basic principles that have been found to be true, and making them adaptable to the conditions of the mid-twentieth century. Yet it must be done, because it is in this way that true progress is made and America becomes stronger day by day both at home and abroad.

Equal Rights for All

Address to the National Convention
of the Anti-Defamation League of
B'nai B'rith

Los Angeles, California, May 6, 1948

WELCOME TO CALIFORNIA for your very important conference. Here you will meet among people who will clearly understand your great objective, because our people are of every racial origin on earth. A million present-day Californians came from foreign lands and over two million of our population are but one generation removed. Many of them, therefore, either have personal knowledge or have information direct from their parents of persecutions and discriminations that caused one or the other of them to leave the land of their fathers for this land of freedom and opportunity.

You will find them in sympathy with the effort being made by the people of good will in all religions and of every racial origin to bring about unqualified recognition of the dignity of the human being—a recognition that carries with it inherent rights to security of person and home, to freedom of religion and of self-expression, to an equal voice in government and to the opportunity to enjoy *all* the benefits of our society. You will find, I hope, that they want this recognition and these rights, not only for themselves, but for everyone.

To say that there has been *no* intolerance in our country would be less than frank. And to the extent that it has been manifested, it has retarded the progress of our country and has diminished our standing before the peoples of the world. But we can thank God that most Americans—Catholics, Jews and Protestants—are trying to eradicate it from our national life. Religious intolerance and hatred is both a mental and a moral sickness. It affects nations as well as individuals, and recently we have seen it utterly destroy the moral fiber of a once great nation. Why the Nazis made the Jew their phobia and how they debauched and ultimately destroyed what once had been a self-respecting nation of ninety million people is for the psychiatrists to determine. But we ordinary people can learn at least three things from the tragic experience: first, that there are no depths of degradation to which intolerance cannot descend; second, that the prejudice which ever lies dormant in the human heart can be fanned to a white heat on a moment's notice; and third, that eventually it is as certain to consume those who practice it as it is to injure those who are the objects of its hatred.

History also teaches us that intolerance is not confined to any nation or race of people. It is not confined to any age. It has come to the surface throughout the centuries under a myriad of circumstances and often under the guise of what is considered by those in power or in the majority to be a worthy cause. But there are times when intolerance is closer to the surface than at other times. I believe we are living in such a time, and that if it were not for the very earnest efforts which are being made by the peace-loving nations toward world co-operation, and the activities of religious groups to stem the tide of intolerance, we would be subjected to far more of it than at present in all parts of the world. I say this because we are still feeling the backlash of two terrible wars which not only destroyed lives and property but undermined morality. The great task before the world today and before the people of this country is to restore confidence in those spiritual and moral values which these two world wars have done so much to destroy.

I presume it is too much to expect that we can entirely eliminate intolerance from human nature in the foreseeable future. It is one of the inherent weaknesses of human nature that have changed little during recorded history. We cannot look forward to the day when we will be able to relax and confidently say that such things are no more. It will always be a fight worthy of our better selves. But if we still believe that the golden rule is a good rule; if we still believe that man is the greatest creation of God; and that life, liberty and the pursuit of happiness are the birthright of every human being, we must also believe that by marshaling the better elements of human nature against prejudice and intolerance we can repress and subdue them through education, through kindly example and through the great force of enlightened public opinion.

This is the job not of some of us, but of all of us. Because intolerance has been directed against the Jews does not make it merely the problem of the Jews. Whenever and wherever intolerance rears its ugly head, it is the job of Americans— not of some Americans but of all Americans—to suppress it.

It cannot be suppressed merely by statutes, because intolerance is too ingenious, too subtle, too diabolical, to be controlled by any written words of statutes or decrees. The only language before which it will fall is the language of the heart.

The American people must keep their hearts open and warm to everyone in our land. We have already opened our hearts, our purses and our energies to helping the stricken peoples of the world without regard to race or creed. We are doing this to create a healthy world in which all people can live in freedom with opportunity and without fear. In wanting this for the entire world there is a large measure of enlightened self-interest for us, because in a world that is less than a healthy world there can be no freedom from fear even for the strongest.

I am proud of what my country is trying to do to make a healthy world. I believe what it is doing is without parallel in human history. Where has it ever been recorded that a great country which has conquered aggression by destroying the strongest and most ruthless armaments in history has immediately turned to the task of rehabilitating the world of friends and foe alike? Our country has done this without demanding reparations, without seeking territory or any other aggrandizement, without imposing its will upon anyone, and merely for the purpose of creating a healthy world in which people can live in peace and work out their own destinies in contentment.

How far we will succeed, no human being can know. There are too many factors beyond our control. We do know, however, that it is almost a superhuman undertaking, and that whatever progress we make will call for all the faith we have in the wisdom of our course, all the strength of our democratic institutions, all the ingenuity and energy of our free economy. To do it we must have the national unity that springs from happy American homes wherein people know in their hearts that we are all doing our best to accomplish the high purposes stated in the preamble of our

Constitution and in the Bill of Rights. Pre-eminent among these high purposes is the elimination of religious intolerance.

It is because I believe that your Anti-Defamation League, your commission and your great fraternal order are working toward that end, and consequently for a happier and more useful America, that I am delighted to be with you this evening.

Penal Reform

"*California's Sentencing and Correctional Methods,*" Address to the National Convention of the American Bar Association, Section on Criminal Law

Atlantic City, New Jersey
October 29, 1946

AT NO TIME since the Reconstruction days following the Civil War have we been confronted with such social and economic dislocations as now exist. These conditions aggravate the problem of controlling crime and delinquency.

As lawyers and public officials, our prime responsibility is the administration and enforcement of law. It is, therefore, the duty and responsibility of those of us gathered here to direct more than ordinary attention to the improvement of the machinery for the prevention of crime and delinquency and the correctional methods employed in the rehabilitation of convicted offenders.

The idea of punishment has not and cannot be entirely abandoned. It should, however, be regarded as only one of the many possible devices for discipline, treatment and ultimate rehabilitation. The protection of society, both immediately and ultimately, is conceived to be the primary purpose of a system of criminal justice. It is obvious that the ultimate protection of society from the depredation of any individual offender can be achieved in only three ways—by imposition of the death penalty, by confinement for life, or by reformation.

In the practical administration of criminal law, more than 95 per cent of all convicted offenders are ultimately released. The dictates of logic demand, therefore, that every resource at our disposal be directed toward the re-education and regeneration of offenders in order that they may eventually assume the responsibilities of citizenship.

Nowhere has this philosophy been completely accepted in practice. It is supported in varying degrees, however, in all jurisdictions.

Perhaps it was inevitable that the administration of criminal justice would develop numerous types of agencies and procedures in the several states. Differences in local conditions, traditions and early history would naturally bring about this result.

In California's case, the early administration of justice was unique. At the time of the American occupation of California in 1846, there were no laws in existence other than such as were upheld by custom. With the establishment of the American military government, the Mexican alcalde system was restored.

The alcalde was the principal municipal officer, who performed duties comparable to the mayors of our cities and held court if a justice of the peace were not available. When there was need for the services of a magistrate, an alcalde was sometimes chosen on the spot and he acted for a single occasion or continued to act according to the pleasure of those who put him into his precarious office. Speedy justice was more desirable than exact justice.

Another form of early California justice was administered by what were known as "miners' courts." When a community of gold rush days was aroused at the commission of some flagrant crime, men were found to act voluntarily as sheriffs. The accused was tried by a jury composed of miners without the aid of a judge. There were no jails. Apparently, the form of punishment meted out did not require their use.

The majority of the settlers were God-fearing and law-abiding men, however, and soon organized local and territorial government followed by a popular movement for an effective state government. In 1849 a constitutional convention was called, and a constitution was adopted the same year. In 1851, an act was passed by the Legislature to provide for the care of state prison convicts, pursuant to which a contract was entered into with private parties for the guarding and safekeeping of the state convicts. There being no prison in existence, the contractors fitted up a prison ship moored in the Bay of San Francisco. Eventually, in 1855 the contractors built a prison at San Quentin.

Penal servitude under the management of private contractors gave rise to many abuses and unwholesome conditions. As a result, the State of California passed an act in 1858 making it the duty of the Governor to take immediate possession of the prisoners and the prison property. The contractors immediately brought suit against the State for forcible entry and detainer. By a decision of the State Supreme Court, the convicts and prison property were restored to the contractors. Thereafter, the State filed an action for the recovery of its prisoners and for the recision of the contract. Only by virtue of a settlement out of court was the State able to recover its prisoners and prison property.

A new state constitution was adopted in 1879. It prohibited contract labor by convicts and also provided for a penal system under the jurisdiction of an administrative board appointed by the Governor. This administrative structure remained in force until 1944. In the interim period, perhaps the outstanding step taken toward modernizing the penal system was the enactment of the indeterminate-sentence law in 1917.

The traditional concept of the court as an agency for the determination of guilt or innocence still stands as the bulwark of American criminal jurisprudence, but during the past generation there has been a growing tendency to question the capacity of criminal courts to prescribe the exact details of the punishment to be administered to convicted offenders.

Wide discrepancies in the sentencing practices of the judges in the fifty-eight counties of the state were the immediate reason for the California indeterminate-sentence law of 1917.

A single state board, separate from the board in charge of the prisons, was empowered to fix terms within the limits prescribed by law, and this has resulted in a more equitable type of justice. This board was also charged with the responsibility for releasing men on parole and maintaining supervision over them during the period of parole.

While this was a vast improvement over the old system, unfortunately it was only a partial remedy. The step still to be taken was the creation and development of a centralized correctional system to include all agencies charged with administrative and quasi-judicial responsibilities.

At the time I became Governor in 1943, the basic law

covering the California penal system had not been changed substantially since 1879. We had two major prisons for men, loosely supervised by a part-time prison board. We had a women's prison, supervised by another part-time board. We had three youth correctional institutions operated by a different Department of Institutions. We had a sentencing and parole board distinct from the Prison Board. We had a Youth Correction Authority without supervision over youth institutions.

There was no over-all Department of Corrections, nor was there any single administrative head to the system. Owing to the confused and conflicting authority of the several state agencies involved, it was impossible for the wardens and superintendents of the several penal institutions to operate effectively. There was a lack of continuity of policy and business administration. Each institution appeared to be going its own separate way, regardless of the effect such a policy had upon the over-all penal problem in the state.

By January of 1944, the need for drastic changes in the system had become so urgent that I called the California Legislature into special session to consider, among other things, a prison reorganization bill. This bill was promptly enacted into law and became effective on May 1, 1944.

The new law created a Department of Corrections administratively headed by a Director of Corrections. Into this department we brought the Youth Authority, handling juvenile institutions and corrections; the Adult Authority, handling adult sentences and paroles; and the women's prison board. This Department of Corrections succeeded to the powers and duties heretofore vested in the numerous independent agencies.

General policy for the whole system is made by all of these agencies sitting as a Board of Corrections, of which the Director is a member. Through this Board of Corrections, the officials and agencies of the department may correlate their individual programs for the adults, men, women and youths, under the jurisdiction of each. It also has the duty of making studies and surveys of all phases of the crime problem and recommending remedial legislation.

The wardens of existing institutions are directly under the supervision of the Director. All of these officials are appointed by the Governor with the advice and consent of the Senate.

It was our idea in California to get away from patchwork on our prison system, and to create once and for all a complete, centralized system. In this work, we received excellent co-operation from the Director of the Federal Prison System. We obtained a director for the California system through an examination to which we invited as many penology career men as we possibly could.

Recognizing the seriousness of the youth problem in California, in 1943 we reorganized and implemented the California Youth Authority. This authority is based on a model act originally recommended by the American Law Institute after consultation with a nationwide committee of lawyers, judges and criminologists.

Although increasing attention was given during the war years to the problem of juvenile crime, the problem itself is no new one. Young people between the ages of fifteen and twenty-one years constitute only 13 per cent of our state population, but a recent California study based upon police and sheriff's records disclosed that during one year more than 40 per cent of all serious public offenses in the state were committed by persons within this age group. In the course of the year studied, more than 50,000 children were arrested, and 22,000 were brought before the juvenile courts of California.

The Youth Authority is composed of three members appointed by the Governor for four-year terms, subject to confirmation by the State Senate. One member is designated Director and Chairman of the Authority by the Governor, and it is his duty to administer the provisions of the act. The Authority as a whole has the responsibility for classification, segregation and parole of young persons committed to it by the courts.

The purpose of the Youth Authority Act is to protect society more effectively by substituting for retributive punishment methods of training and treatment directed toward the correction and rehabilitation of young persons found guilty of public offenses. In California we have also stressed preventive work as well as corrective work.

In brief, the powers and functions of the Youth Authority as they relate to correction and rehabilitation of youthful offenders may be stated as follows:

To make possible more extensive and effective diagnosis, classification and segregation of youthful offenders;

To set up adequate means of custody for treatment of offenders and establish a centralized, integrated, uniform system and procedure for the entire State;

To provide sound and effective means of aftercare and supervision of parole.

The law provides that the court may refer to the Youth Authority any person convicted of a public offense who is found to be under twenty-one years of age. If the Authority believes that any person referred to it can be materially benefited by the procedure and discipline of the Authority and that proper and adequate facilities exist for the care of such persons, it so certifies to the court. The court thereupon commits the person to the Authority.

Although at the present time the law makes it permissive for the courts to refer such cases to the Youth Authority, it becomes mandatory on the courts to make such referrals after January 1, 1948, when our program for expansion of facilities has been carried out.

Whenever it appears to the Authority that a person committed to its jurisdiction is incorrigible or incapable of reformation under the discipline of the Authority, the Authority may return him to the committing court and the court may then commit him to a state prison or a county jail, or make such other disposition as may be provided by law.

For the purpose of carrying out its duties, the Authority is authorized to make use of law enforcement, detention, probation, parole, medical, educational, correctional, segregative and other facilities and agencies, whether public or private, within the state.

The Youth Authority Director may require persons committed to the Authority to perform work necessary and proper to be done by the Division of Forestry, the Division of Beaches and Parks, and the Division of Fish and Game in the Department of Natural Resources, by the Division of State Lands, by the United States Department of Agriculture and by the Federal officials and departments in charge of national forests and parks within the state.

The fundamental and far-reaching change that the Youth Authority Act makes, as compared to the old system of handling youthful offenders, is the provision that instead of commitment by the court to a specific institution such as a jail, reformatory or prison, the commitment of the youth is made to the agency. Once he is committed to the Authority, it becomes the sentencing body, and as a sentencing body the Authority has the power to submit him to any type of treatment, program or placement that it believes most likely to benefit the youth and, in turn, benefit society.

In addition to being a sentencing body, the Youth Authority since 1943 has jurisdiction and control over three correctional schools for boys (one of them a ranch camp), two correctional schools for girls, a diagnostic clinic and four forestry camps.

One of the important contributions of the Youth Authority has been the development of a Delinquency Prevention Program. During the last three years the Authority, upon invitation from local organizations, has made twenty-one county-wide surveys of youth agencies in all parts of the state. Community and co-ordinating councils, teen-age centers and other local activities have received stimulation from this work. Management is left in every case to local agencies, but the Youth Authority continues to keep in touch with more than two hundred such projects throughout the state.

Our preoccupation with the problem of juvenile delinquency has not prevented giving proper attention to the development of facilities for the safekeeping of adult prisoners committed to the state's care and for the training and treatment they need to prepare them for a useful place in society.

In connection with our prison reorganization of 1943, to which I have referred, a new agency composed of three full-time members, known as the Adult Authority, was created to handle quasi-judicial functions relating to the fixing of terms, the granting of paroles and the classification of adult males.

The members of this agency are appointed by the Governor with the advice and consent of the Senate. The law requires that one member of the Adult Authority be an attorney at law, one have practical experience in handling adult prisoners, and one be a sociologist in training and experience.

Certain of the facilities which the members of the Adult

Authority need in performing their functions are provided specifically by the Prison Reorganization Act. One of these is a diagnostic clinic which provides the information on which the Adult Authority may base its decisions. The work of this clinic includes a scientific study of each prisoner, his career and life history and the cause of his criminal acts, and recommendations for his care, training and employment with a view to his reformation and to the protection of society.

In considering a prisoner for release on parole, the Adult Authority has before it a case history which includes commitment date, prior criminal history, circumstances of offense, diagnostic clinic report and recommendations, progress report by the institution officials, reports from the prison psychiatrist and physician, reports from the committing judge, prosecuting attorney, sheriff, chief of police and probation officers, letters from relatives, defense attorneys or other interested parties. In the case of women prisoners, the Board of Trustees of the California Institution for Women has the same powers, duties and functions as the Adult Authority exercises over prisoners.

The reorganization of our prison system has brought about so many improvements in the care and treatment of convicted offenders that it would be impossible to mention all of them at this time. Here are a few:

All institution and staff personnel in the new department have been placed under civil service.

Institution staffs have been reorganized to perform more effectively the complex functions of modern prisons.

An intensive program of in-service training for all employees has been initiated.

A new institution for young offenders who are too incorrigible for the Youth Authority, and too young for even our regular prisons for adults, has been authorized and already opened in temporary facilities pending the construction of a permanent institution.

A competent staff has been organized in the Director's office to supervise institutional functions such as financial controls, personnel management, medical services, building maintenance, inmate classification, record keeping, statistics and prison industries.

Work programs have been reorganized and are being expanded to eliminate idleness in the prisons.

A psychiatric and diagnostic clinic has been established and is making a scientific study of each newly admitted prisoner.

In addition to the institution for incorrigible young offenders mentioned before, the California Legislature, at my request, has authorized the construction of two other new institutions—a medium-security prison and a hospital-type institution for mental cases and chronically ill prisoners.

Further development will be in accordance with an overall master plan for California's correctional system. This program provides for modernization of our old institutions and the construction of new facilities at a cost of approximately $20,000,000. On the basis of laws enacted and funds provided, California may look forward to the completion in a few years of a building program that will provide a well-rounded and diversified system of correctional institutions.

California's institutions were planned and constructed at a time when the population of the state was scarcely more than four million. It is apparent that this extensive building program is made necessary by the vast increase in the state's population as well as by the special social and economic conditions which have followed the war.

With this building program completed, California will have institutions for adult offenders ranging from maximum security at Folsom, through the industrial type at San Quentin, the medium-security type at Soledad, an intermediate reformatory for young prisoners, a specialized medical institution. For juveniles we will have minimum-security facilities and camps under the jurisdiction of the Youth Authority.

Although great progress has been made in the development of our correctional program, the job is not yet completed. We are continuing to study and analyze our future needs. Although antisocial individuals have been identified and segregated for many centuries, we have to admit that, for the most part, society has thus far failed in its efforts toward reformation. However, with the new penological approach, which concerns itself primarily with individual treatment, we look forward to greater accomplishments for the future.

Public Health

Address to the National Convention of
the American Public Health Association

San Francisco, California
October 30, 1951

You HONOR US GREATLY by holding this important convention in our state.

There is no more important problem in the life of the
nation than the health of its people. The fact that progress
has been made on many fronts, and that life has been extended in recent years, furnishes no reason for relaxation. On
the contrary, these advances bring in their wake other problems of equal importance—problems of congestion, chronic
disease, and other problems of the aging.

There is so much to be done, so much to be achieved, that
it is thrilling to contemplate the possibilities. When the
health professions, government and the citizenry grasp the
true significance of a healthy America and join hands en-
thusiastically in achieving it, barriers will be knocked down

and we will make progress rapidly on all fronts rather than piecemeal as we are too often required to do at present.

It is only in the prevention and alleviation of human suffering that the true value of a program such as we now have in California can be found. It is to be found in the prevention of acute communicable diseases; in the help given to children afflicted with cerebral palsy and rheumatic fever; in the early finding and better care of the tuberculous; in safeguarding the population from malaria and encephalitis; in reducing the toll of venereal disease; in helping communities to build more hospitals; in safeguarding the purity of our water and food supplies; in establishing uniform standards of health services throughout the commonwealth; and in training more people for more effective public-health work in more communities.

In expanding the public-health department in this state, we have not attempted or wanted to create a superbureaucracy. We have tried only to follow the wise example of other and older states—and the counsel of the American Public Health Association—by effectuating our program through the local health departments. The state department stimulates and co-ordinates, giving direct service only where state-wide administration is necessary. The local departments deal directly with the people.

This basic policy is administered under the terms of our State Public Health Assistance Act, which provides financial assistance to the organized local health departments and which brought into being the California Conference of Local Health Officers. The Conference establishes the standards that all local health departments must meet in order to qualify for the state subsidy. These standards assure not only that each local health department will offer basic public-health services, but also that its nurses, sanitarians, laboratory technicians and other professional personnel possess high qualifications of training and experience for their work. Our graduated subsidy expresses and implements the mutual interest of all the people of California in public health in every part of the state. It recognizes the fact that health is the most important thing in life.

I do not believe there is any finer example of a successful governmental relationship than that which exists between our State Department of Public Health and the local health departments.

The success which has been achieved in so many parts of our country, and which in a large measure has been stimulated by the American Public Health Association, represents tremendous progress on behalf of the health of the American people. There still are other frontiers, however, that challenge the best in everyone who is determined to establish health of body and mind as the inalienable right of every citizen.

One of these frontiers of public health is the problem of making adequate medical care available to all who need it. As far as facilities are concerned, much has been accomplished in the United States under the Hill-Burton hospital construction act—a program that in California has enabled us to help the local communities in building forty-seven new hospitals and ten health centers. The American people still, however, are confronted with the problem of bringing good medical care within the financial reach of every citizen.

It seems to me that our special concern must be for those who are in the average- and lower-income brackets. The well-to-do can pay for good medical care. The indigent receives it from the public and from the charitable work of the doctors. But the self-reliant workman, who contributes so much to building our country and whose greatest ambition and hope is to raise a good American family, cannot bear the financial catastrophe of serious illness. This is our present-day weakness. It is not sufficient to say that America has developed the finest medical care in the world, even though it is true. We must find a way to make it accessible to our people!

In my own state, I have advocated a program of prepaid medical care as a possible solution. The proposal has been called socialized medicine by some who are opposed to it, and even has been given the ugly name of communism by others. It is neither. Nor is it statism as practiced in Germany, or socialism as practiced in England. I am not enamored of the medical system in vogue in any other country. I have never been and am not now in favor of socialized medicine. I do not believe in socialism. But I do believe in social progress, which has been the hallmark and the glory of the American nation from the beginning. I am convinced we will enter upon a new era of progress in the cause of health when we make it possible for every one of our people to protect himself and his family from the economic disaster of backbreaking hospital and medical bills. I believe it is the responsibility of the states to undertake to help doctors, hospitals and the public they serve in the solution of what, up to the present time, has been an insoluble problem.

I have never claimed that my proposal is the only solution. I have never said it was the best. I have merely said it is my proposal until someone offers a better one. I am convinced that our system is resilient enough to produce the desired result within the governmental, economic and professional concepts of all people who are sincerely interested in the problem. It would be foolish indeed if we were to fall out as to the means. It would be shortsighted and a disservice to the future of America if we were to indulge in rancor instead of approaching the problem in the spirit of doing whatever is necessary to build up our greatest resource—the health of our people.

It is encouraging to know that the American Public Health Association, in its consideration of the problem, has placed emphasis upon the necessity for a high quality of medical care and particularly upon preventive medicine. An emphasis upon preventive medicine is the essential element also in the second frontier on the public-health scene in America. I mean the one that has to do with chronic diseases and the health of our older people. The outstanding present characteristic of the population of the United States is the rate at which the average age is going up, as indicated by the fact that 8 per cent of the total number of people in America today are over sixty-five years old, in contrast with 4 per cent at the time your association was founded seventy-nine years ago.

The public-health profession and all those who co-operate with it are entitled to take a great deal of pride in what has been accomplished in the control of communicable disease and in reducing infant and maternal mortality. The very fact, however, that so much has been done by science to extend the life span from fifty years at the turn of the century to seventy years today has brought forward a new problem— the burden of chronic disease.

We have only recently begun to take cognizance of the toll of chronic diseases and the fact that they cause two-thirds of all deaths in the United States today and the loss of a billion man-days of productivity every year. The association of the progressive aging of the population with this growing burden of chronic disease is no justification for neglect of the problem. Old people still are people. Unnecessary disease and invalidism as they affect these people constitute a challenge to the health profession and to government. The problem is both spiritual and economic. Our older people are entitled to be spared as far as possible from the discomforts and pain of chronic disease, and to have it made possible for them to contribute their productive efforts to society and to be independent. America cannot afford to waste this great resource.

In dealing with the problem of chronic disease, most of the thinking has been in terms of research, medical care, possible rehabilitation, and institutions—with too much emphasis in government on the latter. The time has come to put more effort and planning and money into prevention. The position your association took four years ago to the effect that the basic approach to chronic disease must be preventive expresses a fundamental truth and should be our guide. In California we undertook an approach to the problem of chronic disease just two weeks ago in a conference at Sacramento when two thousand of our citizens got together to consider this and the other problems of the aging. More than four hundred leaders in the health professions and lay groups participated in the sections which were devoted to physical- and mental-health problems, and among the concrete proposals they formulated the emphasis was on preventive measures.

The health professions and the voluntary agencies are entitled to all the help government can give them in their efforts to find better methods for the prevention of chronic illness and the disabilities resulting from cancer, heart disease, diabetes and arthritis. This co-operative effort will lessen the ever increasing burden of suffering and expense that weighs now so heavily upon society and the individual.

The third frontier of public health that still requires our attention and the utmost of our effort is the problem of the permanently disabled. The first approach has been to provide minimum cash benefits during periods of disability, but the more fundamental solution must be to restore as many of the disabled to productive and happy lives as may be possible through the combined efforts of science and government.

If we can make progress in these three great areas of public health, our country will be a happier place for all the people in it. I realize that I have not been telling you anything during these past few minutes that you do not know far better than I. I have wanted to make it clear, however, that as far as I am concerned the health professions and the great voluntary agencies are entitled to all the help and all the cooperation that government can give in working toward the most important of social aims—the health of our citizenry. I appreciate this opportunity to share my thinking with you respecting some of the major problems of public health. I pledge my continued interest in your work, and I extend my best wishes for a successful convention and one that will add a great deal to the contribution you have been making throughout the years to social progress in our land.

The Republican Party

Lincoln Day Address, Middlesex Club
Lincoln Day Dinner

Boston, Massachusetts
February 12, 1952

THIS IS A RARE PRIVILEGE for me, coming as I do from the other side of the continent to address this oldest of Republican clubs in the nation. It was generous of you to invite me.

I wish all our Western Republicans could enjoy the thrill I feel tonight being in New England, where freedom on this continent was born and cradled and brought to maturity as the United States of America. It would strengthen their faith in our nation. It would fortify them in their resolution to guide it by Republican principles. It would increase their appreciation of the significance the birthday of the father of our party has to the nation, to ourselves and to those who will follow us, so long as the Union to which his life was dedicated exists.

These Lincoln Day dinners held by Republicans from the Atlantic to the Pacific and from the Canadian to the Mexican

38

border have become one of the finest traditions of our party. They afford an opportunity to review the past and survey the future, an opportunity for introspection and soul searching. They make it possible for us to commune with one another to determine whether we are following the principles of Lincoln or are merely using his hallowed name as a trademark of the party. Or stated in another way, whether we are using the occasion to popularize the party or to rededicate ourselves to the principles for which he stood; whether, like him, we will at all times "dare to do the right."

If Lincoln were in Washington today, he would feel that our country is moving from uncertainty to crisis, as he did when he came to Washington in 1861. He would sit in his chair as his image sits in our great memorial to him in that city. He would be in deep soul-searching thought. His kind and perceptive eyes would be attempting to pierce the future. He would be sad because after so much bloodshed we had not achieved a durable peace. He would believe that our country is in as grave danger as it was in 1861. His absorbing concern would be for the future of the country, as it was then. He would say as he said in that year, "I am exceedingly anxious that this Union, the Constitution, and the liberties of the people shall be perpetuated in accordance with the original idea for which that struggle was made, and I shall be happy, indeed, if I shall be a humble instrument in the hands of the Almighty . . . for perpetuating the object of that great struggle." His great anxiety would be for its perpetuation in a world that is half slave and half free. His first, last, and constant concern would be for our country, and he would do now as he did then, subordinate everything to its preservation.

In his mind's eye, he would view the Communist aggressions in every part of the world and translate the danger that flows therefrom to the security of the country. He would

loathe Communism and its world-wide conspiracy. He would
be for an affirmative program that would prevent its aggression. He would stand in that cause with every nation that
desired to be free, and he would look upon such an association of nations as we in our Republican Party platform of
1948 described the United Nations to be—"the world's best
hope in this direction." He would recognize that each
country standing alone could not withstand aggressions of
the Communist war machine. He would understand that
many of them, being small and poor and weak and dispirited
by having been overrun in two world wars, could do very
little alone to repel such aggression. He would have com-
passion for them as he did for the downtrodden in our own
country in his day. He would give solace to them in their
distress. He would cheer them in their efforts to remain free.
He would help them to remain free. He would inspire them
and ourselves for the cause of freedom—freedom not just
for some, but freedom for all.

His heart would be for peace always, but his hands, his
strong body and his clear mind would fight if necessary to
achieve it. He would be neither pugnacious nor vacillating,
but he would be determined and he would persevere in
spite of discouraging reverses, bigotry or personal abuse. And
with his devotion to the cause, his forthrightness of approach,
his fairness of speech and action, his rugged honesty and his
humanity, he would be a leader both at home and abroad in
the cause of freedom. There would be no guile in his proposals. He would be frank with us and with the world. There
would be neither overtones nor undertones to his actions.
They would be understood by all. He would invite all Americans regardless of party to work with him for peace and he
would indeed abandon politics at the water's edge. He would
not demand perfection either in human nature or in organizations, but he would labor with all his might and under-

standing for co-operation and collective action both at home and abroad.

With the introspection of which he was capable, he would review the past, he would profit by previous mistakes, he would look into the future and, to use his own language, would discharge the obligation to transmit our heritage "to the latest generation that fate shall permit the world to know."

He would be greatly saddened at what he could see: our uncertain position in a turbulent world; our defenses, only recently so secure, now weakened to the point of great danger; our rearmament program faltering; duplication, over-lapping and obsolescence besetting our government; daily scandals degrading it; taxes mounting to heights that destroy incentive; inflation rampant and withal an attitude of complacency on the part of the party in power that constitutes a road block to real progress. He would set his mind to changing these conditions.

He would perceive that some of the inequalities of his day still existed and that the freedom of opportunity he strove for was not yet a reality. And he would say as he said then that ours "is a struggle for maintaining in the world that form and substance of government whose leading object is to elevate the condition of men . . . to lift artificial weights from all shoulders; to clear the paths of laudable pursuit for all; to afford all an unfettered start, and a fair chance in the race of life." He would also repeat what he said a few days before his inauguration:

I hold that while man exists it is his duty to improve not only his condition, but to assist in ameliorating mankind; and therefore without entering upon the details of the question I will simply say that I am for those means which will give the greatest good to the greatest number.

41

Why do we presume to look through Lincoln's eyes and speak with his lips about conditions of our day? Because he is not of any particular time. As Stanton said at his death-bed, "Now he belongs to the ages."

It is often difficult to appraise the great figures of history according to the standards and the problems of our own day. So many of them were creatures only of their own times. They were able to successfully adjust themselves to a particular set of circumstances, but their contribution was limited in time and space.

Not so with Lincoln. His greatness lies in the fact that he was able to live by fundamental principles and to maintain a spirit applicable to all times and under all circumstances. His clear understanding of democracy and its application to mankind in his or any other day has never been better expressed than when he said: "As I would not be a slave, so I would not be a master. This expresses my idea of democracy. Whatever differs from this, to the extent of the difference is not democracy."

His practice of homely virtues, his devotion to justice and his consideration for others are the things that have made his memory not only a treasure of patriotic sentiment, but a source of practical guidance for the nation.

There is so much that could be said about Lincoln, but it must be remembered that no words of ours could add a single inch to his stature. However, we can, by following him, add to our stature. And that is the purpose of these gatherings.

What we should talk about, then, is our need today for the great faith that was Lincoln's—faith in his party, faith in his people, faith in his country, faith in God. And for us today also, faith in all the nations of the free world, and faith in all those people of the slave world who yearn to be free.

We need faith as Americans have needed it in every crisis of history. The faith we need is the faith to do the things that should be done for the betterment of our people—not just some of our people, but all our people. We should not be afraid to speak of or advocate the "general welfare." Lincoln had no such fear and the Constitution says it is the fundamental purpose for which our government is formed. We should not shy away from the term "civil liberties." The Constitution was not ratified until assurance had been given that they would be guaranteed in the Bill of Rights. And Lincoln said, "The fight must go on. The cause of civil liberty must not be surrendered at the end of one or even a hundred defeats." The term "social justice" is not an evil one. It comes to us from the Holy Bible.

"Social progress" is nothing to run from. America is the creature of social progress, a monument to its power and beauty. It has been through a process of social progress that we have grown to leadership in the world. It was Lincoln's creed, and those who confuse it with socialism today are indulging in the kind of thinking that Lincoln described as not being able to distinguish between a horse chestnut and a chestnut horse.

We shouldn't be afraid of "collective bargaining," or of "social security." Both have been advocated by our party for years.

None of these are odious words or terms. They are of respectable origin and they represent the faith that our forebears had in their ability to govern themselves. They are the essence of Republicanism. They are the opposite of socialism. Collectively they represent America's way of avoiding collectivism and strengthening our enterprise system so all can compete on equal terms.

The Declaration of Independence proclaiming that all men are created equal and are entitled to "life, liberty, and the pursuit of happiness" was the greatest forward step in social progress in political history.

The dedication of our government to "promote the General Welfare," the Bill of Rights, the Fourteenth and Fifteenth amendments, the enfranchisement of women, free education, the protection of property, our concern for the unfortunate, and the recognition of the true dignity of labor are all hallmarks of social progress unequaled in other parts of the world.

It must be apparent to everyone that we have not yet achieved perfection, and that as long as there are inequalities to be adjusted, unfortunates to be helped, we must maintain our faith in being able to use our institutions for improving the conditions of our citizens.

It was not the fear but the faith of our fathers which has carried us where we are today. Should America ever grow overly cautious and fail to live boldly in her effort to achieve an ever richer life, she will have entered upon her decay.

We must move on as research and science develop new fields of promise and hope. We must not change merely for the sake of change, but we must not fear it when it will serve to refresh and to renew our society and to keep it young and eager and adventurous. In the cause of our marvelous growth industry has not hesitated to destroy great works that it might erect new ones at great cost, if it would even in a small way improve the quality of its products or decrease its cost. That policy has given us the industrial leadership of the world. Government must not lack the courage and the wisdom of industry nor fear to grasp the conditions of a more nearly perfect life.

To those who are afraid of social progress because it might lead to socialism, it can safely be said that no straighter road to socialism could be made than to have any President or Congress try to stop social progress. There are some in our party who would like to turn the clock back. There are many more Democrats who would like to convince everybody that all Republicans would do so if they had the opportunity. If either of these groups succeeds, our party will no longer be a party of the people and will be doomed permanently to minority status.

We should not be disturbed by the fact that our opponents use the same terms and have programs for their accomplishment; neither should we be perturbed because extremists have distorted their meaning and have attempted to misuse them. We know what they mean. We have advocated their advancement for years. We must have our own programs and move forward in the spirit of evolution and progress. This was the approach of Lincoln, who frankly said, "I am a slow walker, but I never walk backwards."

We need have no fear that advocating these things will erase the distinction between our opponents and ourselves. We cannot permit anyone to pre-empt the principles or programs upon which a better life can be achieved for our people. No one owns a good idea. The better it is, the more it should belong to everyone. Our recent platforms have stated and reiterated:

Our goal is to prevent hardship and poverty in America. [*1944*]

No problem exists that cannot be solved by American methods. [1944]

We have followed these statements of principle with an espousal of programs for the solution of the major social problems of our day. I find it profitable from time to time to read those platforms. They are enlightening. They are convincing, to me at least, that we have not departed from the principles of Lincoln.

45

One of the opening statements in our 1948 platform quotes Lincoln as follows:

"The dogmas of the quiet past are inadequate to the stormy present. The occasion is piled high with difficulty and we must rise with the occasion. As our case is new, so we must think anew and act anew."

The platform concluded with this prayer:

Guided by these principles, with continuing faith in Almighty God; united in the spirit of brotherhood; and using to the full the skills, resources and blessings of liberty with which we are endowed; we, the American people, will courageously advance to meet the challenge of the future.

These sentiments are equally applicable to 1952, and within their framework the problems of our day can be solved. We can and we must "think anew and act anew." We must look ahead, not back. We must show that the Republican Party does not need to state its case in terms of invective, ridicule or negation. We have the know-how and the gumption to make a frontal attack. It is our duty to the public. It is what is expected of us.

This is a time for boldness. A bewildered nation, depressed by confusion and fear, is looking for leadership. To give it is the solemn obligation of our party, an obligation which tonight in the name of Lincoln we pledge ourselves to redeem.

And lest there be any doubt about whose job it is, I close with this quotation from Lincoln:

I appeal to you to constantly bear in mind that not with politicians, not with Presidents, not with office seekers, but with you is the question: "Shall the liberties of this country be preserved to the latest generations?"

46

The Hopes of Man

Address of Welcome to the Founding
Delegates of the United Nations

San Francisco, California
April 25, 1945

THE PEOPLE OF CALIFORNIA are highly honored by your presence. We are profoundly grateful to the United Nations for the unity which has pushed the war to a stage that makes timely such a conference as is now being opened. We share with you the full realization of the importance and the solemnity of the occasion.

You are meeting in a state where the people have unshakeable faith in the great purposes which have inspired your gathering. We look upon your presence as a great and necessary step toward world peace. It is our daily prayer that the bonds of understanding forged here will serve to benefit all humanity for generations to come.

We here on the Pacific Coast of the United States of America are fully aware of the special recognition you have given us. Ours is a young civilization—a civilization that has made its greatest development during the lifetime of men now living. Many of you represent nations which are not only ages old, but which have for centuries been making the struggle for a better world, the struggle in which we are now all joined. It is a double compliment to us, therefore, to have our young and hopeful segment of the world chosen as the drafting room for a new era in international good will.

We recognize that our future is linked with a world future in which the term "good neighbor" has become a global consideration. We have learned that understanding of one another's problems is the greatest assurance of peace and that true understanding comes only as the product of free consultation.

This conference is proof in itself of the new conception of neighborliness and unity which must be recognized in world affairs. The plan to hold this conference was announced in Yalta, halfway around the world, only two and a half months ago. Yet in spite of all the tragic events of the war, including the sad and untimely death of our own President, it opens today here in San Francisco, on schedule, and without the slightest interference with the greatest military undertakings in all history.

Unity has created the strength to win the war. It is bringing us ever closer to the end of world conflict. This same strength of unity, continued and cultivated here, can be made to develop a sound pattern of world affairs with a new measure of security for all nations.

It is in the spirit of neighborliness that we join you in advancing tolerance and understanding, the tools with which we are confident a better and a happier world can be built.

It is in expression of this spirit that I, as Governor of California, welcome you.

Address Commemorating the Centennial of the Discovery of Gold in California

Coloma, California, January 24, 1948

THIS IS THE CENTENNIAL which the people of California have long looked forward to—the centennial of the discovery of gold. The discovery of gold was not the first important event in the history of this state. Our roots go much deeper than that. But this centennial recognizes the finding of gold here in Coloma by James Marshall on January 24, 1848, because the discovery set in motion a chain of events that had nationwide significance and started the phenomenal growth of California that has continued to this day.

The centennial also emphasizes the transition from a sleepy pastoral age on a lonely and isolated frontier to the dynamic and populous California of today. Thus was this Western country changed from a wilderness with only a few little settlements to a great American state of ten million people in the short period of one hundred years. Just how short a period that is can be judged from a simple story the newspapers carried a few days ago. This story reported the death of a pioneer woman, a native of Clarksville in this county. She was born during the gold rush years almost a century ago. Everything you see in California came into being during her lifetime. This is indeed a miraculously short time for the accomplishments which are so apparent to everyone who knows our state today.

Long before the discovery of gold here, California acted as a magnet for treasure seekers. Out of the dim past came legends of fabulous wealth here known to the explorers and adventurers the world over. It attracted them in some strange way from all the maritime countries of the world. The Portuguese Cabrillo as early as 1542 discovered the Bay of San Diego and explored our coast. His body is said to be buried on one of our channel islands. The Englishman Drake in 1579 explored our coast within a hundred miles of this spot. Vizcaino, the Spaniard, followed in 1602. Then in 1769, after a century and a half of complete darkness, came the rugged Portola and the kindly Father Junipero Serra to found San Diego, Monterey and the twenty-one missions which brought Western civilization and the Christian religion as far north as Sonoma.

In January 1848 there were here, exclusive of the native Indians, probably fifteen thousand people from many countries. About six thousand of them were Americans. The American flag had already been raised in Monterey and other settlements in 1846, but there was no American government in California. Those who came here fashioned their own government. They were a sturdy lot. Among them was Johann Sutter, an intrepid Swiss who had visions not of gold, but of a pastoral empire in the Sacramento Valley, and with him was his partner for some purposes—James Marshall, an American. In the course of their operations they built here in Coloma the little lumber mill where Marshall accidentally discovered gold—the gold that changed life so greatly in the West and in a very short time brought not only California but the other Western states into the Union as dynamic units of a nation destined to do great things for humanity. It is an event worthy of commemoration. It thrills every Californian and furnishes the background for the colorful years that followed in such rapid succession. It has left a permanent imprint upon the life and character of our state.

It has long been the custom of mankind to commemorate those dates in history which record the achievements of great men or the great accomplishments of groups of men. It is man's way of giving recognition to those qualities of personal leadership, those courageous achievements and group sacrifices which occur in the development of our civilization and in the growth of the nations of the world. It is man's way of re-experiencing the aspirations, the hardships, the sorrows, sentiments and happiness of his fellow countrymen of an earlier age, that he might better understand his fellow men of this age. And what is equally important for the welfare of humanity is that it is man's way of pausing in the frantic rush of daily affairs to look forward as well as backward, upon the better world he is ever seeking to build.

As we look into the future there is much for us to learn from the adventurous lives of our pioneers. These men and women had vision. They had an appreciation of what this great Western country held for people who desired to achieve. They had the indomitable courage to face the rugged elements of nature. Above all, they had the courage to face the great unknown.

And the reason they had this courage was that they had faith—faith in God, faith in mankind, and faith in themselves. It was by this faith that they lived during the trying years in which they established an orderly society out here on the Pacific Coast.

Today we face a future that is as uncertain as that of our pioneers. The world is chaotic. In many countries, greed and hatred and aggression are superimposed on the destruction of war, hunger and disease. Nations are striving to maintain their independence and people are crying out for freedom. If they are to succeed, if we are to be able to help them succeed, we all need as never before the fundamental qualities of the pioneer. We must have a vision of world peace. We must have the will to achieve it, and the faith to meet the uncertainties of the future with confidence and courage.

Of all the people on earth, Californians should have an abundance of this faith and courage. We have been blessed beyond comparison during this first century of our existence. We have taken improvidently from our forests, our streams and our valleys, yet our natural resources, greater in value many times over than the gold which was taken from these mountains, still await further development. The water of this American River, when stored at Folsom and other dam sites, will develop everlasting wealth in the fertile valleys below. It will light our cities, turn the wheels of industry, irrigate our fields, and preserve our wild life for those who love these mountains. Floods will be prevented. This wealth will not diminish through the years as did the gold deposits discovered by James Marshall one hundred years ago today. It will continue to enrich our state as long as the winter snows fall on the high Sierras and melt in the spring.

Because this Gold Discovery Centennial Day gives us an opportunity to honor those who pioneered our state and the inspiration to look forward to another century of progress, it is an important day in the history of California. I am happy to share it with you.

Address of Welcome to the Delegates
of the Japanese Peace Treaty Conference

San Francisco, California
September 4, 1951

I WELCOME YOU to California. I greet all of you in the spirit
of the great cause that brings you here. I extend to you on
behalf of our people the hospitality of a cosmopolitan state
that is enamored of the world and believes that through
world co-operation it can be made for all a better place in
which to live. Here you will find true recognition of the fact
that peace is a way of life which leaves no room for hatred,
greed, rancor or arrogance. Here you will find a belief in the
humanitarian motives that prompted this conference, and
agreement that the only peace which is lasting is that which
comes from mutual recognition of the dignity of the individual, the equality of mankind and the sovereignty of all
peoples.

The very atmosphere of this place in which you start your
conference is one of peace. This building is dedicated to
those who lost their lives in the cause of freedom and peace.
Here also the Charter of the United Nations, with its solemn
pledge of world peace, was signed by most of the countries
which you today represent. This city was named for and has
emulated a saintly man of peace, a man who lived in poverty

53

while performing acts of great charity for the poor, the downtrodden and the afflicted.

Our state from the beginning a hundred years ago has received people from every section of the globe; and today, with people of every racial origin and culture, we live in peace and harmony, hoping that the world will soon be able to do likewise. Every effort made to accomplish that result is in the interest of humanity. This conference is an important step forward in that direction. We hope and pray for its success.

From the far parts of the world you have gathered here today to consider a treaty of peace, a treaty involving the future of millions upon millions of people, a treaty between peoples of variant social customs, history and economy— peoples who, organized as nations, collectively and individually possess the requisite strength to influence all the world for generations to come.

Specifically we call this proceeding the signing of a treaty between the Allied Powers and Japan. To me it is much more. It is the prototype of what must be done time and time again if we are to build the workable structure for permanent peace which was envisioned here in this very same hall when the United Nations was created. It is an exemplar of benevolence and realism never yet consummated between victor and vanquished.

It has been said many times during recent weeks that never before in history have victors been so magnanimous with the vanquished, that never before in history have the conquered been so encouraged to regain their normal status of dignity and self-esteem. To me such an attitude on the part of victors not only is much to be desired, but is essential. Progress in this world has never been made by grinding people down. Progress comes only when people have opportunity and it comes then only in proportion to the degree to which they are able to satisfy their basic needs.

In the Orient today, food in quantities to provide health, growth and physical vigor, and employment which offers opportunities to possess a home, a cow and a piece of ground are two of the essentials. These are basic needs which must be recognized else present distress be extended to additional millions. These needs cannot be supplied merely by a treaty of peace. They will be supplied only when we encourage leadership which can and will dedicate itself to the task of building up agriculture to the point where industry can have its development and where programs are initiated to maintain a balance between agriculture and industry in the interest of both rural and urban life.

It has been my privilege during the past few weeks to visit Japan, and I have returned convinced that if given the opportunity and sympathetic assistance, Japan is in a position to contribute mightily to the type of leadership which the cause of peace now needs so desperately in the Far East. Never have I seen people who were more industrious, more ingenious in the adaptation of their limited resources to their needs, more patient in working out their problems, or more cheerful in assuming their personal and national burdens.

As I saw millions tilling the soil, other millions restoring the industrial potential of the nation, and still other millions of children carrying their books to and from school, all of them intent on these peaceful pursuits, and cheerful in the performance of them, I became convinced that Japan wants to be at peace in a free world. More than that, I became convinced that Japan is ready for peace, the kind of peace that is to be under consideration here, a peace that will restore her sovereignty, her self-respect, her opportunity to prosper and a place among the free nations of the world.

California is happy to have one of its great cities shoulder the mantle of a world capital today and serve as your host on this occasion.

We welcome you, one and all, as individuals for your own worth. We welcome you as representatives of your government, with which we want so much to be friendly. We welcome you as messengers of peace and good will in a very troubled world.

II

Liberty and the Law

Addresses

of the Chief Justice

*Address at the Eighty-sixth Charter
Day Exercises of the University of California*

Berkeley, California, March 23, 1954

"IT IS GOOD TO BE HERE"—if I may use the words made famous on this campus more than a half century ago by one of our illustrious presidents when he arrived here to build toward the destiny of the university. And may I say by way of emphasis, without detracting one whit from his fervor on that occasion, that his joy in being here and his hopes for the future of our university could not have exceeded my own today.

I have not been away from California for a very long time nor have I been more than a ten-hour airplane trip from Berkeley. Neither did I leave here against my wish—far from it. But when one considers such a sudden change in jobs as I made, in both character and locale, taken together with the leaving behind of members of the family, friends, worthwhile institutions such as this, the dropping of problems that had been challenging through the years, the abandonment of uncompleted programs for the development of our state, while at the same time having a strong desire to help in keeping California the finest place on earth in which to live

—such a combination of dislocations makes Washington at times seem to be a long way from California.

I want to say I am proud of my university today as I have always been since I carried logs and boxes to the bonfire in this Greek Theater for the freshman rally so many years ago.

I am proud of our great President Bob Sproul, who has not only brought the university to a position of eminence among the centers of culture in the world, but who has also kept it in that honored position year after year until it has come to be recognized as such everywhere.

I am proud of the great faculty that has made the phenomenal progress of a young university possible. When I refer to a great faculty I do not refer only to those professors who have by long years of service attained the pinnacle of their profession, nor only to those who have already received the accolade from industry, business or government. I speak rather of the total number, now reaching into the thousands, who are, with the same devotion as their elders, doing the research, teaching classes, counseling students, correcting papers, and who, in the aggregate, integrate the manifold activities of the university into one great program—a program of expanding the area of knowledge in every direction by pushing boundaries farther and farther, by raising horizons higher and higher and by passing knowledge on and on through succeeding college generations into the stream of everyday life. It has been a truly great faculty by this measuring rod, a great company of scholars dedicated to the search for truth. It has had its critics at times as have most of our institutions in these turbulent days, but it has come through as gold from the burning, honest in its research, sound in its teaching, dedicated to the finest ideals of the profession, loyal to the spirit of the institutions Americans hold dear, and courageous in its adherence to truth and right.

I am grateful for the fact that as a student many years ago

I was the beneficiary of the devoted services of some of those men whose names now appear on tablets around the campus —Benjamin Ide Wheeler, Charles Mills Gayley, Henry Morse Stephens, John Galen Howard, Armin O. Leuschner, Andrew W. Lawson, and a host of others. What a galaxy of stalwarts they were.

I am infinitely more grateful, however, for the fact that my six children have had the privilege of studying here under worthy successors to those stalwarts. Now, in order that you may not conclude that I have been too provincial or too fierce in my attachments to this particular campus, I report to you that while two of these youngsters graduated here, two of them are indebted to the Los Angeles campus, and the two remaining to Davis.

Lest some of you leave with the impression that this was a by-product of my late so-called nonpartisan administration of state affairs, I hasten also to report that this was a matter of individual choice by them and that each of them is as rabid in his campus and athletic loyalties as I am. As a matter of fact I am looking forward to the day when I can even the count with my two U. C. L. A. daughters. On the Saturday preceding the national election in 1952, after their Bruins had administered an unbrotherly trouncing to our beloved Golden Bears, they sent me what I still consider to have been a totally unnecessary and undaughterly telegram saying, "I hope your candidate does better than your football team."

To return for a moment to the faculty. I want to say that given the opportunity, it can and I am sure will take this university to heights not yet envisioned. I say "given the opportunity" because in some parts of the country and in some circles, people are asking the question, "Can we afford all of these educational programs?" Some of these people, I am sure, have answered the question in the negative before asking it. To me, however, it seems obvious that so long as we spend only seven tenths of one per cent of our national income on higher education, both public and private, and over thirty times that much for national defense, we had better be thinking about expanding higher education in order to develop programs that will enable the peoples of the world to live together understandingly in peace and security.

California cannot afford to be without one of the great universities of the world. Its university must be striving always for pre-eminence, not for personal or local pride, but in order to better serve our state and nation in a turbulent, bitter, changing and confusing world. We must have additional knowledge and greater wisdom if we are to find our way out of our dilemmas. We have not acquired sufficient of either to solve the problems of our own day, much less the unseen problems of any future day. It will never be adequate merely to pass on to youth the knowledge of any given day. We cannot lower our sights in these troublesome times. We must never run short of intellectual ammunition. American universities everywhere must continue to strengthen their programs. They must also strengthen their zeal. There should be renewed vigor in all of them for free investigation and faithful research by the unfettered minds of free American scholars. In this resurgence our own university should be in the front row.

We have unique opportunities and even greater responsibilities in California. We are still pioneering here the newest civilization on earth. Our working tools are our citizens of every racial origin on earth. Our culture is based upon many others. People have come here from every quarter of the globe seeking opportunity. Opportunities are here in abundance and we can make of them what we will. We can minimize them by tying ourselves solely to the past and the present with their proven limitations, or through free investigation and faithful research we can open new horizons which will make available to us the knowledge of the past and the ingenuity of our own day.

When our university was chartered eighty-six years ago there were 500,000 people in the entire state. Today there are over 12,000,000. We are told and have every reason to believe that in 1970 there will be 20,000,000.

In our first graduation class there were eighteen graduates. Last year there were 9,976. Shortly after the war when we were giving our service men and women their belated education we had a class of 13,642. Educators and population analysts warn us that before 1970, when the World War II babies and postwar babies become of college age, the enrollment will double. There will be great minds among them. It will be the business of the university then, as it is now, to develop such minds so they will come to the top to serve humanity, our government and our economic system. To the extent that we fall short of doing this we will be short-changing the cause of freedom, because free government, free enterprise, indeed all the facets of freedom, are inseparably connected with the opportunities that come from free investigation and faithful experiment.

I have no fear that we shall fail in our responsibilities. The people of California love their university. They rely upon it. They trust it. Legislatures of the past have, almost without exception, recognized its needs and met them. I do not doubt this, and future Legislatures will do the same. But it is not fair to rely solely on the Legislature's understanding of university problems. They too need a sustaining hand. We citizens of California, fathers, mothers, alumni, must have a vision for our university and a determination that it shall always be second to none.

We gather in this beautiful Greek Theater typical of the culture and beauty of an ancient civilization. Some of you from the seats you are sitting in are able to look out through the Golden Gate to the Pacific Ocean, which harbors on the shores of its great basin more than a billion people of many races, cultures, and nations. Some of them have civilizations that were old when Europe was young. We know them and they know us only slightly. Lack of knowledge has isolated us from one another throughout the centuries. But at the present time the entire basin is in a state of renaissance. Like ourselves, all these people have new ideas, new hopes, new ambitions. They are seeking new friendships. They will find them one place or another. How much better that they should find them here instead of behind the Iron Curtain.

There has been an age of the Persian Gulf, an age of the Aegean, an age of the Mediterranean, an age of the Atlantic. Do not the signs of the times point to an age of the Pacific? Can we say it has not begun? At all events, much of the history written during the lives of our children and their children will be of the history of the Pacific.

California is as favored in its possibilities for peaceful, wholesome and purposeful relations with the peoples of the Pacific Basin as any state or nation on earth. But we must know them. How better could we cement those relationships than by having a great understanding university that knows the Pacific Basin as we know the Sacramento Valley and by an exchange with its people of knowledge, ideas and students? In this world that is shrinking in size day by day, there is no solvent for our problems with our neighbors except wisdom born of the kind of knowledge that can be acquired through universities.

As we try to look into the future, and try we must, whether we are thinking in terms of domestic or international problems we must realize that our basic problem is to learn to live understandingly with the peoples of the world, at peace and in security. To do this we need not only a broad base for higher education. We need also to stir the imagination and the genius of our greatest minds through the services of great universities.

I am happy in the knowledge that on its eighty-sixth birthday my university, the University of California, is manfully shouldering its part of that responsibility, and in the belief that it will continue to do so as long as "our sturdy Golden Bear is watching from the skies."

"The Blessings of Liberty," Address
at the Second Century Convocation of
Washington University

St. Louis, Missouri, February 19, 1955

It is a thrilling experience to participate in the opening session of this Second Century Convocation of Washington University. The time, the place and the cause to which the convocation is dedicated make it an occasion of major importance. The campus of Washington University, enriched by a hundred years of devotion to the highest ideals of education and by the contribution of its thousands of alumni to the good life in America, provides an ideal place to reflect upon the blessings of liberty. To do so at a centennial celebration where the experience of the past, the events of the present and aims for the future can so appropriately be brought into balance adds greatly to the content of the occasion.

The times in which we are living are not normal times. Powerful forces are at work in the world—both to preserve liberty and to extinguish it. The interplay of hope and fear, belief and doubt, determination and frustration keeps the affairs of mankind and the minds of people in a state of turbulence—a turbulence that destroys perspective and clouds the vision. Such times call for constant reflection and reappraisal. In the atmosphere of these surroundings where men and women have devoted their lives to the pursuit of truth throughout an entire century, we can more effectively detach ourselves for the moment from the complexities of everyday life in order to determine what our heritage of liberty is and what we are doing today to preserve it for our children and for those who come after them.

It is imperative that we do this. Notwithstanding the contributions of patriots through the centuries, the farsighted wisdom of the founding fathers or the written guarantees of the Constitution, liberty is not necessarily our permanent possession. Both external and internal pressures constantly assail it. It is axiomatic that every generation, to keep its freedom, must earn it through understanding of the past, vigilance in the present and determination for the future.

It is easier to know how to combat a foreign enemy who challenges our right to these freedoms and thus prevent a sudden collapse of the things we hold dear than it is to subject ourselves to daily analysis and discipline for the purpose of preventing the erosion that can with equal effectiveness destroy them. I say "easier" because Americans have never hesitated to make the choice between liberty and death. Normally we can rely upon our representatives in government to keep our defenses sufficiently strong to enable us to ward off outside attack, but we cannot delegate to any or all of our governmental representatives the full responsibility for protection of our freedoms from the processes of erosion. Such protection can be had only through an understanding on the part of individual citizens of what these freedoms are, how they came into being and whether their spirit dominates our institutions and the life of our country. The protection I speak of is that sense of strength and comradeship which flows from national unity, buttressed by freedom of thought, of expression, of nobility and of participation by all in the life and government of the nation.

I have no doubt it seems strange to some people that we take time to discuss such things almost two centuries after the adoption of the Constitution and its Bill of Rights. There are some who regard our freedoms merely as their birthright which they may simply take for granted. There are others who would never shrink from the loss of little freedoms—by the other fellow, of course. And there are also those who would procrastinate until the deluge. The fact remains, however, we do have a battle today to keep our freedoms from eroding, just as Americans in every past age were obliged to struggle for theirs. Many thoughtful people are of the opinion that the danger of erosion is greater than that of direct attack. I do not mean to suggest—nor do they, I am sure—that outside of the totalitarian menace any substantial group of our citizens would willfully destroy our freedoms. But the emotional influences of the times, coupled with the latent suspicion and prejudice inherent in human nature, are capable of threatening the basic rights of everyone, unless those emotions are controlled by self-discipline, community spirit and governmental action.

A few days ago I read in the newspaper that a group of state employees—not in Missouri—charged with responsibility for determining what announcements could be posted on the employees' bulletin board refused to permit the Bill of Rights to be posted on the ground that it was a controversial document. It was reported that the altercation became intense, and that only after the Governor in writing vouched for its noncontroversial character was the Bill of Rights permitted to occupy a place along with routine items of interest to the state employees. And this happened in the United States of America on the fifteenth day of December, 1954, the 163rd anniversary of our Bill of Rights, declared by proclamation of President Eisenhower to be Bill of Rights Day.

It is straws in the wind like this which cause some thoughtful people to ask the question whether ratification of the Bill of Rights could be obtained today if we were faced squarely with the issue. They inquire whether we are as united today in defending our traditional freedoms as were the American people in asserting them during the first years of constitutional government in the United States.

My faith in the sober second thought of the American people makes me confident that it would now be ratified. On the other hand, I am not prepared to dispute with those who believe the issue would provoke great controversy.

Have we not had enough controversy over teaching in and the conduct of our colleges and schools, both public and private, to warrant the inference that an effort would be made to curb freedom of speech and thought in that important segment of American life?

Have not sufficient doubts been expressed concerning the rights of individuals to invoke their constitutional privilege against self-incrimination to justify the belief that the proposed adoption of this safeguard against tyranny might provoke heated discussion?

Does not the suspicion that has attached to lawyers who represent unpopular defendants indicate some departure from the constitutional principle that every person charged with crime is entitled to be effectively represented by counsel?

Are there not enough short cuts advocated—and too often practiced—in our time-honored legal procedures resulting in what we called a denial of due process of law?

Have there not been enough invasions of the freedom of the press to justify a concern about the inviolability of that great right?

Departures from the letter and spirit of our constitutional principles are not the product of any one person or any one group of persons. They are more properly chargeable to the entire body politic; to the suspicion, hatred, intolerance, and irresponsibility that stalk the world today; and also to a lack of appreciation of the age-old struggle of mankind to achieve our present-day blessings of liberty. Government—whether national, state or local—is not the sole culprit in this matter. For it does not operate in a vacuum. In the last analysis it only reflects the mores, the attitudes, the state of mind of the dominant groups of society.

How do we come to have a Bill of Rights, and what is its significance in the history of this nation?

The Bill of Rights, which became part of our fundamental law in December 1791, does not by any means define all our rights. Many of our rights are to be found in the original Constitution, and others are formulated in later amendments.

The Bill of Rights did not originate the rights which it guarantees; there was at the time of its adoption not a single novel idea in it. It did summarize in a striking and effective manner the personal and public liberties which Americans 164 years ago regarded as their due and as being properly beyond the reach of any government, old or new.

The men of our First Congress knew, as we may be in danger of forgetting, that each element in the Bill of Rights was a painfully won acquisition. They knew that government must be neither too strong nor too weak; that whatever form it may assume, government is potentially as dangerous a thing as it is a necessary one. They knew that power must be lodged somewhere to prevent anarchy within and conquest from without, but that this power could be abused to the detriment of their liberties. Confronted by this paradox, they turned to the experience of their forebears for counsel.

The English people, in their long struggle to control the monarchy founded by William the Conqueror, hit upon a happy solution: government should remain strong for its proper ends, but its strength should be kept within clearly defined limits. It became the consensus of the English people that certain acts should be clearly understood by all to be beyond power of government, and illegal if committed by any of its agents. Here we have the basis of the Anglo-Saxon legal and constitutional tradition.

The first great document in this tradition was the Magna Charta of 1215. There was little new in Magna Charta. It merely recorded the rights which had been asserted, with varying success, against the Norman monarchy during the previous century and a half, and needless to say, there were reactions and backslidings in the five centuries that followed. But in the main the movement was forward, toward the accumulation of a body of well-established liberties and immunities enjoyed by the trueborn Englishman.

The century or so during which the British colonized America was especially important in the development of British constitutional rights. A full century before Madison rose in the First Congress and proposed our American Bill of Rights, the British Bill of Rights had already come into being. It was the culmination of generations of struggle against the arbitrary government of the Stuart dynasty in England.

In the course of the eighteenth century, the question arose whether the residents of thirteen American colonies were trueborn Englishmen and as such entitled to the traditional liberties and immunities enjoyed in the homeland. Since the King and the Parliament of Great Britain were resolved upon giving a negative answer to this question, the colonies decided, in the year 1776, that the time had come to make a fresh start, and to adopt a Declaration of Independence.

In one sense, the Declaration is a lineal descendant of Magna Charta. But in another sense, it is a very different sort of document, a characteristic product of the Age of Reason. Instead of appealing to royal concessions and traditional immunities, it takes its stand upon self-evident truths, the laws of nature, and unalienable rights. It was a new turn in human history. It was an experiment which had never been attempted. It is still on trial.

Our Revolutionary forefathers had had their fill of royal governors, and of George III and his ministers, and so they forgot for a time one of the great lessons of constitutional history: that government must be strong for its proper ends. Many of the new state constitutions set up a hobbled and ineffectual executive branch. Our first attempt to create a national government, the Articles of Confederation, provided for no executive at all. Our attempt to operate under a weak government barely got us through the Revolutionary War. The return of peace began a drift which, all clear minds perceived, was toward anarchy. The inevitable and timely reaction brought about the Federal Convention of 1787, by which our present Constitution was submitted to the American people.

To the American people, the Constitution was a new and permanent legal basis for their government. They wanted nothing left to conjecture. They insisted upon concrete rights being set down in black and white. If government was to be strengthened, the more apparent became the need to delimit its proper powers, and to itemize the immunities which its citizens ought to enjoy. And so, directly upon the establishment of government under the Constitution, the First Congress submitted the Bill of Rights to the states.

Such, in the most general kind of way, is the process by which we acquired our Bill of Rights. If you have not read its provisions recently, I urge that you read and reread them.

They were never more important. The Bill of Rights contains only 462 words and can be read in only a few moments, but from the American viewpoint it embraces the wisdom of the ages as divined from man's struggle for freedom throughout civilization.

The liberties thus written into our fundamental law have not gone unassailed in the course of our national history, for men in office are still men. Whether men derive their authority from hereditary right or from popular election, they remain prone to overstep constitutional limitations and invade legal immunities. Periods of domestic dissension and of foreign war are especially liable to produce tendencies to disregard established rights in the name of national safety. Often the tendency persists after the danger which provoked it has passed away, and at such times Americans who cherish these rights have had to fight to vindicate them. The French Revolution, and the deep cleft of opinion which it brought about in our country, led to the notorious Alien and Sedition Acts of 1798. When Thomas Jefferson succeeded to the Presidency three years later, he set free all those who had been imprisoned under what he regarded as an unconstitutional statute. Our Civil War saw the tendency to substitute military for civil tribunals which the Supreme Court rebuked in the famous case of *Ex parte Milligan* in 1866. World War I was followed by a wave of repressive measures, such as mass arrests without benefit of habeas corpus, which were strenuously opposed by the libertarians of that day. In our time, we have seen the greatest of wars give way to a decade of chronic tension and crisis, in which it is to be expected that new encroachments upon traditional liberties may have to be countered.

I have suggested that if there has been damage done to our traditional rights it has been accomplished by a process of erosion. Are the privileges and immunities summoned

73

up in our Bill of Rights in danger of loss through subtle changes in our climate of opinion? Is distrust of our fellow countrymen wearing away our traditional concept of the innate dignity of man?

These questions call for constant and intense exploration far beyond the limits of this discussion; but because we are here on the campus of a great university, I would remind myself and you that if our other rights are to be of value to us we must first have the untrammeled right to search for the truth in institutions such as this, and then to teach it in accordance with the dictates of conscience. If that right should ever fail, so will our other blessings of liberty. That is precisely what has happened to people in other parts of the world, and in our time.

But I do not wish to end on a mournful note. Nor do I wish to suggest that our liberties are about to be lost. Erosion may have begun in some respects but the fabric of our liberties is still far from undermined.

Surely the America that sent twelve million men into a world war to preserve freedom everywhere will not allow its own freedoms to be frittered away. Surely the America that has poured out its substance to rehabilitate the free world, and even our former enemies, so that they can resist tyranny, will not willingly pass on to its children less freedom than it has itself enjoyed.

It has been sagely remarked that men more frequently require to be reminded than informed, and I hope that we may all join in the good work of reminding each other of how much we have to lose, and how heedless we would be to lose it.

With a strong belief in the wholesomeness of our objectives and the courage to defend our freedoms, I have no doubt we shall preserve our heritage.

Faith, the Apostle tells us, is the substance of things hoped for, the evidence of things not seen. Faith in America confirms the hope that we shall preserve for our children all that our fathers, by the way of clear thinking, firm resolution, patient endurance and willing sacrifice, secured for us; that our heritage of liberty will not dwindle but increase; and that we will prove worthy of what we have so abundantly received.

It is such faith, I believe, that brings all of us together today to consider the blessings of liberty.

Address at the Centennial Celebration for Robert M. La Follette, Sr.

Madison, Wisconsin, June 10, 1955

You do me great honor in permitting me to speak at this official centennial of the birth of your most distinguished citizen. I appreciate your hospitality the more because of the intimacy of the meeting in the presence of members of the La Follette family, old companions and lifelong believers in his principles of public morality; and because the meeting is sponsored by this learned and patriotic Wisconsin Historical Society. Lastly I appreciate it because it is being held in your capital city where, as Governor, many of his great accomplishments were made and because here at your great university he not only received his intellectual inspiration but he met and married his mate, companion and lifelong source of inspiration.

In such surroundings and under such auspices, one who did not have even the privilege of a personal acquaintance with the honoree must be doubly conscious of the hospitality that is being shown him in permitting him to participate.

I am not here to recount the life and works of Bob La Follette. I take it that none of us are here for that purpose.

The people of Wisconsin and particularly those who are here know his life, chapter and verse.

It was so inseparable from the growth and the development of your state that his good works are everywhere around us today: your great university, the majesty of the law as represented by your stately capitol, the institutions under which you live as contained in the journals of the Legislature; and above all the abiding affection that people still have for his memory.

What I do believe we are here for is to rekindle the flame of his memory, in gratitude for his long and distinguished public services and because his dynamic principles and his fighting spirit are as needed today as they were in his heyday.

It was not my pleasure to have known him. I saw him on the platform on occasions and while still a college student I once heard him from the gallery pour out his heart from the floor of the Senate.

But I feel I knew Bob La Follette. I acquired something from him, as did other Americans who perhaps never saw him but who believe that the substance of our government is to be found not in its form but in the eternal principles upon which it is based, and which if preserved must be fought for by courageous men and women in every generation. "Let fools for forms of government contest; that which is administered best is best."

It has been my great privilege to serve the public most of my adult life. I too had the responsibility as Governor of my state to make our institutions serve the best interests of all the people. I know the pressures that Bob La Follette found it necessary to resist and overcome in order to give our democratic process the broad base it must have to serve its purpose. Every governor knows those pressures because they are in every state capital. And they will probably always be there, because, as long as we have free government, of necessity we will have pressures of selfishness, greed and intolerance as well as those for the common weal.

There are times in the life of every public servant when the feeling of frustration becomes almost overwhelming. It is at such times that we come to know and appreciate the indomitable spirit of souls like that of Bob La Follette. It was in that way I came to know him, although I assumed my first public office almost at the precise time of his death thirty years ago.

Some historian has referred to our state governments as forty-eight laboratories for the development of our institutions. I believe that to be true. The older states, of course, built the foundation for our system, but it remained for Bob La Follette, one of the last of our log cabin statesmen, to turn the searchlight upon our social problems and to grind out with mortar and pestle the answers to them. And he suffered the same treatment that courageous men of vision in all ages have suffered. He was called a radical, a disrupter, a socialist, a subverter, and perhaps the only reason he was not called a Communist was that that term had not then been popularized as a term of opprobrium. But he was a life-long Republican, steeped in the tradition of that party which was born in this state the year after his birth. He believed in the party system.

But he believed in parties and his party in particular as a party of the people—farmers, workmen, small businessmen —not as an oligarchy of dominant interests.

He believed in private property:

Property, whether the modest home of the artisan or farmer, or the great fortune of the masters of finance, if it be honorably acquired and lawfully used, is a contribution to the stability of government, as well as to material progress.

He believed in the private ownership of utilities, but he believed in regulating them for the public good:

The owners of railroads and the holders of railroad securities must be protected in all of their rights. They must not be wronged in any way. They are entitled to such remuneration as will enable them to maintain their roads in perfect condition, pay the best of wages to employees, meet all other expenses incident to operation, and in addition thereto enough more to make a reasonable profit upon every dollar invested in the business. To preserve all these rights, they are entitled to the strongest protection which the law can afford.

He believed implicitly in our system, but he believed it belonged to the people, that it should not be shackled and that every hindrance should be removed from it in order to enable it to progress so that it might produce a better life for every man and woman and their children. This is the way he stated the issue:

The supreme issue, involving all others, is the encroachment of the powerful few upon the rights of the many.

These were the undergirding principles of the Wisconsin Idea of which he was the father. These were the motive power in his laboratory of human problems.

How detestable those experiments of his were to some people of his day. How commonplace they are now. How much a part of American life they are:

The direct primary, giving control over government to the people instead of to bossism.

The Corrupt Practices Act, preventing the pollution of the election process.

79

The establishment of a comprehensive civil service to destroy the spoils system.

The registration-of-lobbyists act—not to prevent them from functioning but to bring them out in the open because, as he said, "Evil and corruption thrive best in the dark."

The equalization of taxation between the individual citizen and the powerful corporate interest. "Equal and just taxation," he said, "is a fundamental principle of republican government."

An inheritance tax and a graduated income tax based on the ability to pay.

The regulation of utilities to prevent indirect and unjust taxation from burdening the people.

The right of workingmen to join unions and bargain for their rights. He was determined there should be no submerged class of industrial workers.

The health and safety of the people through pure-food laws and compensation for industrial accidents.

The development of the university and a sound system of general education.

These were the ingredients of the Wisconsin Idea. It is for these things Bob La Follette was called a dangerous radical. Was it a radical program? Is it radical today?

While it has found acceptance in the hearts and minds of most Americans, I am sure there are those who still believe it is radical, and are nostalgic for the so-called "good old days." There are still among us those who would call it socialism, those who refuse to make any distinction between socialism and social progress, those whom Lincoln described as being unable to distinguish a horse chestnut from a chestnut horse. There will be such in every generation. That is why under our system every generation must fight for the kind of society and economy it desires to have, and the standards of the government it is to live under.

If the Wisconsin Idea was radical it was so only in the sense that freedom itself is radical. And it was so considered when the founding fathers brought our nation into existence. It was radical only if the idea of government "of the people, by the people, for the people" is radical.

But also it must be remembered that the party of Bob La Follette—the Republican Party—was considered radical when it was founded. Think of it. It proposed to prevent the spread of slavery, to open up the great public lands of this Western country to settlement by families, and to give the average man a greater stake in society and in his government. That was radicalism when Bob was born.

Bob's difficulty came from the fact that he took the principles and platforms of his party at face value. He believed it was a party of the people and he determined to make it serve that purpose. But he realized that these things could not be done overnight. He wanted it done through reform. He wanted it all to come by peaceful means. He was not in a hurry to push the nation into reforms for which it was not prepared. On the contrary, he said, "Everything worth while takes time, and the years teach us all patience."

Again he was squarely in the American tradition, with its reliance on the idealism and innate reasonableness of men. He had an old-fashioned faith in the sovereign power of reason in human affairs.

But pre-eminently, Bob La Follette was a dissenter—a dissenter in the finest sense of the word.

He did not dissent through mere obstinacy. He dissented in righteous indignation when he thought the objectives of our government were being subverted. He satisfied what is said to be the acid test of dissent, namely the ability to get

itself accepted finally as the truth. In this respect no states-
man in our history has succeeded better. I have often won-
dered if he, as a boy, heard of the advice given by Disraeli
to a young politician. When asked what he could best do to
serve the public well, Disraeli replied: "Associate yourself
with a just, but unpopular, cause." Often his voice sounded
as one in the wilderness because the most successful and
most respectable in the nation were carried away with the
doctrine of laissez faire. They believed that our new industrial society, if not interfered with by government, would
lead to Utopia. Bob reminded them that merely an abundance of materials did not represent true progress; that progress implied the progressive enlightenment of the people, the
humanization of our institutions and the free application of
intelligence in the evolution of society. He reminded them
that in their enthusiasm for material gains they were break-
ing with the ideals of an earlier day. It was often a thankless
task. But it needed to be said, and he said it. He was called
wrong, shortsighted and unfair. But no one ever called Bob
La Follette dishonest. And when he died in 1925 he enjoyed
the respect of everyone.

How important it is that we keep alive this type of dissent
in America! It is as important now as it was then. We must
test all of our public actions by dissent. The majority does
not always discover the right answer until it is so tested.

The term "Fighting Bob" to the uninformed might con-
note a man in uniform, a general or perhaps an admiral.
Particularly would that have been true in days gone by, when
the history of nations was written in terms of their wars,
their most glorious achievements in terms of battles won
and their heroes in terms of conquerors of other people.
Not so with Bob La Follette. He was a man of peace—not
a pacifist but a fighter for peace. He fought for peace with

the same steadfastness of purpose that he fought for other things. He was not cowed by the majority view. He was satisfied to live with his own conscience.

Yes, he was scathed for it, but he died with the respect of everyone.

The day before yesterday I participated in the unveiling of a statue of a former Chief Justice in the rotunda of our national Capitol. There were the images—two from each state—of the most beloved men and women of American history. I noticed that the vast majority of them were civilians rather than military men—statesmen, social workers, philanthropists, scientists and humanitarians of various description. They were citizens of peace. In the forefront of these was the statue of Fighting Bob La Follette, most beloved son of Wisconsin. Instantly my thoughts flew back to the turbulent days of his career, and then it occurred to me how understanding Americans are on sober second thought, how willing they are to make amends for harsh appraisals made in times of crisis, and how the objects of their lasting affection are those who have tried to make life more rewarding for everyone. I could not help noticing how stalwart Bob La Follette appeared in that company.

And today to see the affectionate regard in which he is held in his own state, thirty years after his death, produces a thrill of pride and a feeling of well-being.

I trust that one hundred years from today the people of Wisconsin will gather in this same spot to rekindle the flame of his memory. His accomplishments should then stand out in even bolder relief. The need for his understanding of people, his devotion to their interests, his fighting faith in our free institutions, will be equally as great as it is now.

It will give the people of Wisconsin then the same feeling of well-being that we have today.

83

Response to an Address by the President of the United States at the John Marshall Bicentennial Ceremonies of the American Bar Association

Philadelphia, Pennsylvania
August 24, 1955

MR. PRESIDENT:

Your presence here and your challenging words give to our bicentennial observance of the birth of the great Chief Justice a significance it could not otherwise have—a significance that is emphasized by your own personal leadership in the present world-wide struggle between the forces of freedom and totalitarianism.

This public rededication of the bar and bench of America to constitutional principles, joined as we are by the Chief Executive of our nation, will be heartening to everyone who believes in the force of law rather than the law of force.

To lawyers the place where we humbly perform this rite is hallowed ground.

To us it represents more than any other place in our broad land of vision, the wisdom, the courage and the independence of those who conceived for us a perpetual union under free institutions.

This was the seat of the Continental Congress when it adopted and proclaimed to the world our Declaration of Independence.

It was from Independence Hall that the Liberty Bell did "proclaim liberty throughout all the land unto all the inhabitants thereof."

It was here that the founding fathers wrote the Constitution which has enabled us to develop from the "ugly duckling" of the nations of the world to a nation of 165 million God-fearing, peaceful, happy people who wish for all others the same blessings we enjoy.

It was here that the three co-ordinate branches of our government first met and demonstrated toward each other that self-restraint and respect that are so essential to the development and permanence of our government.

It was here that the giants of those early days established relationships which developed not only a system of government but also a way of life.

It was here that the Supreme Court of the United States first met and started to attach to the bare bones of the Constitution the sinews and flesh that have made it a living, growing, dynamic organism of freedom for ourselves and for those who are to follow us.

It was here that John Marshall, expounder of the Constitution, gave up this life in the thirty-fifth year of his Chief Justiceship after making a contribution to constitutional government unparalleled in history.

It was here that the Liberty Bell tolled its last melodious notes as his body was carried affectionately to the dock for passage to his native Virginia. As though it also was ending an epoch of American life, it split open and like Marshall became a mute but eternal symbol of constitutional government.

Today we recognize these symbols as being inseparable.

The controversy which raged around Marshall during his long career quickly subsided at his death and he soon became judged by the rule of reason rather than by the rule of perfection. Today we appraise him as we do a lofty mountain peak—not by the crevices, jagged rocks and slides that are so apparent at close view, but by the height, the symmetry and the grandeur it acquires in the perspective of distance.

Thus viewed, John Marshall stands out as a colossus among the giants of his time.

Like the other leaders of his day he exhibited a strong will born of violent experiences. The dangers of frontier life which he encountered as a child, his sufferings as a Revolutionary soldier, his experience as an advocate before inept courts and his contacts with a weak national government all conspired to give him a ruling passion to build a government sufficiently strong to assure both stability and freedom. That he made a greater contribution to this cause than any other member of our profession is now common knowledge. In doing so he left us a heritage of both freedom and stability; but he could not perpetuate either stability or freedom. Every generation must earn those things for itself.

Our problems in this regard are as pressing as they were in the days of John Marshall and call for the same devotion to constitutional principles. A dedicated bench and a militant bar are the natural leaders in such a cause.

Without an independent judiciary there can be no freedom. Without a militant bar to assert in court the constitutional rights of individuals regardless of how unpopular those assertions might be at the moment, such rights become merely "sounding brass and tinkling cymbals."

Insistence upon the independence of the judiciary in the early days of our nation was perhaps John Marshall's greatest contribution to constitutional law. He aptly stated the controlling principle when, in speaking of the Court during his tenure, he said that they had "never sought to enlarge the judicial power beyond its proper bounds, nor feared to carry it to the fullest extent that duty required." That is precisely the obligation of the judiciary today. Self-restraint and fearlessness are always essential attributes of every branch of our government.

In Marshall's day the paramount problem was that of implementing the national government so that it would have the strength to perpetuate itself and command respect both at home and abroad. Through the years that has been accomplished to a remarkable degree. We are now a great nation united in thought and action. Freedom has been preserved. Marshall's goal has been achieved.

But we now live in a different kind of world—an ideological world which disagrees violently on the proper relationship between the individual and the state and in which there is a constant struggle for the minds and hearts of people. We and other free countries are endeavoring to demonstrate that freedom and dignity for all constitute the only sound basis for world peace.

In such a gigantic struggle where the eyes of a critical world are constantly upon everyone, the power of example is far more forceful than that of precept.

If the world is made to see that the provisions of our Constitution guaranteeing human rights are living things enjoyed by all Americans and enforceable in our courts everywhere, it will do much to turn the tide in our favor and, therefore, toward peace. Thus interpreted and applied, the constitutional principles of John Marshall will take on even added luster through the years.

No higher mission could be the lot of the bar and the bench of America than to achieve this purpose, and we grasp the opportunity. No more appropriate place than this could be found for accepting such a mission. No assemblage could give greater assurance of our good faith than this which includes the President of the United States. Let our acceptance of this mission then be recognized as our renewed and solemn pledge of adherence to constitutional principles in America's quest for "EQUAL JUSTICE UNDER LAW."

YOU HONOR ME GREATLY. To permit me to speak in the intimacy of this gathering on an occasion of such importance to all of you is an honor which I do not take lightly, and the very recognition of that honor causes me to have some diffidence in accepting the responsibility. The very intimacy of the occasion gives me pause, because here I see the people who conceived the idea and brought your university into being. I see those who are presently guiding its activities. I see those dedicated people who are devoting their lives to training the youth who pass this way. I see the young people who are here imbibing the spirit of the university and the wisdom of the ages. I also see those who worked with him for whom your university was named through the years of his service on the Court of which I am now a member. All of you know much more about him than I do. You are so steeped in his philosophy, in his faith in democracy and in his great vision for America that you can expect little, if anything, from me concerning your patron that is not already known to and appreciated by you.

But perhaps on one theory my selection for this purpose can be justified. It has been said that people more often need to be reminded than informed. And that, it seems to me, is the spirit of anniversaries, both religious and profane. It is our custom to gather annually in various capacities to honor the memories of those who have been greatly responsible for our spiritual and governmental heritage. We hear little that is new in our present-day celebrations of the birthdays of Washington, Lincoln and Jefferson, but they still serve a purpose in rekindling the spirit evinced by those men and in recharging our own minds with the high purposes that impelled them to contribute so much to the society in which we live and to the institutions which guard our wellbeing. They afford us the opportunity to say in unison, "Lest we forget." I believe in anniversaries for that purpose; particularly do I believe in centennials. There is something about a century as a measuring stick that does not seem to apply to other units of time. Considering the whole span of history, it is, of course, a short measuring stick, but it is sufficiently long to allow for objectivity and at the same time is not so remote but what all of us can have a sense of belonging to it.

Every century is different from the others. Each has its own special significance. The one in which Louis Dembitz Brandeis lived was one of the most dynamic in history and the nation to which his life was dedicated was the most dynamic in that century.

Since 1856 this country has grown from twenty-five million people to 168 million. In that period forty million people from every nation on earth have migrated to America and have thrown themselves into the development of our Republic and into the shaping of our institutions. In that time we have peacefully undergone both industrial and social revolutions, and it must remain a matter of wonderment how so many people of so many different races and diverse cultures could mold themselves into one nation of free institutions.

These centennials afford us an opportunity for taking inventory of that transformation, and for striking a balance between our blessings and our corresponding responsibilities. I believe it is in this spirit that we celebrate today the one-hundredth anniversary of the birth of this great, simple, kindly, prophetic American, Louis Dembitz Brandeis.

He believed implicitly that blessings and responsibilities go hand in hand. He often said that "responsibility is the great developer." His great concern for our country was that our vast material wealth, our inherited freedoms, together with soft living, might cause us to become spiritually weak to the point where we would value luxury more than liberty and thus permit our freedoms to crode. He saw the seeds of this evil sown throughout the land, and he determined that so far as he could influence American thought and life, he would not permit our material prosperity to become the cause for falling into comfortable servitude. He prepared himself as an individual to meet it. He taught the dangers of it to every youth he contacted. He dissented against its spread—in his private life, in his public utterances, in his advocacy in our courts, and as a Justice of the Supreme Court. He so interpreted the Constitution of the United States that it could not be used to advance that evil.

While still a young man, at the height of his wealth-producing capabilities, he decided to live a life disciplined to few needs in order that he might not be obliged to depend upon large retainers to maintain an accustomed standard of living. He moved to a smaller house; he changed his manner of living to Spartan simplicity. He restricted his practice of the law for profit to a part-time basis and devoted the major portion of his time to public causes. He fortified his

faith and practice in the religion of his fathers, and he became the confidant and counselor of every earnest young
person with whom he came in contact. Thus devoted to spiritual and public causes and freed from the motive of personal
gain, he increased his hours of labor, strengthened his ideals
and deepened his convictions about the destiny of our nation. Thus he and his family lived the last fifty years of his
life. During all those years, he not only sustained his own
faith but maintained faith in others in the advancement of
public causes. When those around him were dubious because of public apathy, he told them:

*There is in most Americans some spark of idealism, which
can be fanned into a flame. It takes sometimes a divining rod
to find what it is; but when found, and . . . disclosed to the
owners, the results are often most extraordinary.*

By nature he was a plain man. His concepts were simple,
and like his fellow Kentuckian, Abraham Lincoln, whom he
resembled in both stature and facial appearance, his concern
was for the freedom of the individual and particularly of the
weak and defenseless. He was a reformer by nature but he
depended little on emotion—almost entirely on facts. His
concept of free institutions was a unitary one—that political
freedom is inseparably connected with economic and social
freedoms, that there can be no political freedom without
the others, that the opportunity of everyone to compete in
our society on equal terms and to make full use of all his
talents is inherent in and essential to our American system.
He did not profess to be the "friend" of any group or class.
He believed that every individual should have a place in the
sun and that our nation should never become, as others have,
a place where the rich grow richer while the poor become
poorer.

In the evening of his life he said: "I have no rigid social philosophy. I have been too intent on concrete problems of practical justice." Yet no American of his day had a more profound philosophy. In the context of one of those concrete problems to which he referred, he had this to say:

The makers of the Constitution undertook to secure conditions favorable to the pursuit of happiness. They recognized the significance of man's spiritual nature, of his feelings and of his intellect. They knew that only a part of the pain, pleasure and satisfactions of life are to be found in material things. They sought to protect Americans in their beliefs, their thoughts, their emotions and their sensations. They conferred, as against the government, the right to be let alone—the most comprehensive of rights and the right most valued by civilized men.

There is nothing in his long career as a lawyer, as a Justice of the Supreme Court or in his private life inconsistent with this. His whole life was devoted to keeping the shackles off people. He insisted that each individual was entitled to room to grow to the full stature of his own personality. He fought bigness in the cloak of monopoly all his life because he believed that monopoly impoverished human personality. That belief was not merely for contemplation; it was a fighting faith. He defied the status quo and all the powerful influences in our society that sought to preserve it. He did not shrink from the repercussions of this defiance. When lesser men faltered, he persisted. He never compromised. He endured slander and vilification with serenity. In later years, he accepted recantation of this vilification with equal serenity.

Most of his life he was cast in the role of a nonconformist to the conventional views of the day, but there was nothing negative in his make-up. Every disagreement carried with it a solution. He premised everything on facts, in the assembly of which he was not surpassed. The logic he employed to reach his conclusions rested on his faith in the individual. That faith made him a liberal; his passion for facts made him a conservative. It can be said of him perhaps more truly than of any other American in his century that he was a composite of liberalism and conservatism. No American has been more devoted to our system of private enterprise than he was. Yet no American fought harder against the evils that permeated it. He did as much to change the thought of the nation and the outlook of his government concerning American life as any person of his time. Fortunately, he lived to see his philosophy become that of his government. He proved not only the right to dissent in America but also that dissent can be constructive. In the words of his great friend and fellow dissenter, Mr. Justice Holmes, "In ages to come men will be marching to the measure of his thought."

His hopes for the future of America were intertwined with the education of our youth—not only in the great cities but in remote parts of the country. Realizing the importance of the hinterland in its influence on the thought of the nation, he advised ambitious young people not to flock to the great metropolitan centers for opportunity but to remain and work in the vineyards they loved and understood.

I am sure Justice Brandeis is happy today in the knowledge that this great university dedicated to his principles and named for him has made such rapid progress in the eight short years of its existence. I am sure he is happy in the knowledge that we who are gathered here today, thinking only in terms of the welfare of our country, are expressing our determination to carry on these principles. Since he passed to the Great Beyond, the world has passed from the Mechanical Age which he understood so thoroughly to the

Atomic Age of which none of us are yet able to grasp the significance. But I have no doubt that were he with us, he would not change his principles or his approach to life in any degree. He would believe and act according to the belief that, over the long haul, universities such as this will have more power than the H-bomb and that disciplined minds will eventually have a more penetrating effect than guided missiles. He would still believe in personal freedoms—the right to think and believe and to speak even in dissent. He would still believe that monopoly results in a "curse of bigness." He would still believe that the best in American life should be available to all rather than to a favored or fortunate few and he would still fight for those beliefs. He would still see growing evils to dissent from, and he would still be urging young people to dedicate their lives to his concepts. To the extent that we refurbish our own ideals to further those principles, this one-hundredth anniversary of his birth serves a noble purpose and gives added assurance of the lasting greatness of Brandeis University, which bears his name.

"A Way of Life," Address at the
Veterans Day Brotherhood Luncheon
of the National Conference of Christians and Jews

New York, November 12, 1956

THIS IS a very happy experience for me. To have been able
to join with you in dedicating a room in your Building for
Brotherhood to the memory of my illustrious predecessor
Charles Evans Hughes was an experience that I prize very
highly. This great American, although only recently departed
from our midst, is already legendary in our Court. For intellectual capacity, human understanding and administrative
prowess, he has not been surpassed in its history. Every
member of the Court, and particularly those who served with
him—Black, Reed, Frankfurter and Douglas—would be
happy to take over this particular assignment. Their affection
and admiration for him, acquired through daily association
over a period of years, would have fitted any of them better
than me to speak of his great force for good in the life of
our nation. But because I am his successor, three degrees
removed, it becomes my privilege to express the pride we all
feel in the fact that he turned his powerful mind and his

warm heart to the great cause of founding this National Conference of Christians and Jews. It is not the least of the many important causes to which he directed his great abilities.

It is still too early to determine what effect this organization launched by him, Roger Williams Straus, S. Parkes Cadman, Carlton J. H. Hayes and Newton D. Baker is destined to have on life on this globe. But I am sure everyone in this room, at least, will agree that it has potentialities far greater than that yet achieved. I say this without minimizing in the slightest degree the splendid work done by Dr. Clinchy and his associates in the past twenty-nine years. They have done exceedingly well and they deserve a much broader base upon which to build the world brotherhood to which their lives are dedicated.

This meeting brings back for me many happy memories. It was a great many years ago—more than twenty-five, I am sure—when Dr. Clinchy and his associates, a reverend Catholic father and a Jewish rabbi, came to my home in Oakland, California, to explain the then new organization of Christians and Jews. A few of us, none of whom according to my memory were clergymen, met for luncheon at the Athletic Club to discuss it. We were Protestants, Jews and Catholics. All of us were friends, but we had never before discussed religion with one another. I remember how strange it seemed for us to be doing so then and how warily we approached the subject on that occasion. Dr. Clinchy left with our promise to meet again to explore the possibility of establishing a local organization of Christians and Jews. We did meet and soon our diffidence about discussing such matters gave way to enthusiasm. We perfected an organization, and it is prospering to this day. I want to say to you that it helped our community greatly, and that in the intervening years many worthwhile things that otherwise would have been doomed to failure were accomplished because of the understanding achieved by these men of different faiths.

Many other American communities—three hundred of them—have enjoyed the same experience, but for every such one there are ten that have not. It would be a wonderful thing if cities all over the world were to form such organizations, and I applaud every effort to bring that result about. But there is still a job of equal importance to be done here at home in bringing about the understanding that destroys bigotry and substitutes for it co-operation and good will. It was the recognition of this need that caused Chief Justice Hughes and his associates to sponsor this organization. His words are as true today as they were then:

Rancor and bigotry, racial animosities and intolerances are . . . the deadly enemies of true democracy, more dangerous than any external force because they undermine the very foundations of democratic effort.

He felt this deeply. His early religious training, his inherent sense of justice, his wide experience as a lawyer and his global experiences as Secretary of State convinced him that the great need of our country and the world was a spirit of tolerance. Contemporaneously with the founding of this organization, in addressing the American Bar Association in one of his most solemn addresses he said:

The most ominous sign of our time, as it seems to me, is the indication of the growth of an intolerant spirit. It is the more dangerous when armed, as it usually is, with sincere conviction. We justly prize our safeguards against abuses but they will not last long if intolerance gets under way. The just demands of liberty are not to be satisfied even by a free

98

and uncorrupted right of suffrage. Democracy has its own capacity for tyranny. Some of the most menacing encroachments upon liberty invoke the democratic principle and assert the right of the majority to rule—freedom is in danger of being slain at her own altars if the passion for uniformity and control of opinion gathers head. . . .

He had been thinking deeply about these things. He had followed closely and with the deepest anxiety the fever of intolerance that swept over our country soon after the end of World War I. Those were the days of the Ku Klux Klan and of unbridled action of the government against people suspected of radicalism. It came to a crisis in this state in 1920 when your Legislature denied five of its regularly elected members the right to take their seats because they were Socialists. This was too much for the sense of justice of Charles Evans Hughes. He started a crusade in the Bar of this city to defend the rights of those men. At the request of the Bar, he sought leave of the Legislature to represent them in their effort to take their seats. So wild was the hysteria that Charles Evans Hughes, former great Governor of New York, former Justice of the Supreme Court of the United States, former standard-bearer of his party for the Presidency of the United States, and by all odds the most distinguished citizen of the state, was denied the right even to testify before the Judiciary Committee of its Assembly. He did not quit. He filed a powerful brief demonstrating the justice of his cause. As might be expected, it fell on deaf ears in the Legislature, which proceeded to expel the Socialists and also to outlaw the Socialist Party. On the other hand, it had a profound effect throughout the country. An eminent constitutional writer said, "The Assembly was past saving, but the nation was saved." Of all the public services performed by Charles Evans Hughes none was on a higher plane or called for more courage than this. It was one of his finest hours in a long life of distinguished public service.

It was not difficult for him to take such stands. He did so instinctively. With him, justice, fair dealing, tolerance and equality were not mere intellectual pursuits. They represented spiritual values without which our institutions could not survive.

I have recalled the incident of 1920 and the importance Hughes attached to it, because history has a strange way of repeating itself. Unless we keep such acts of intolerance in our mind's eye, freedom can be endangered even in our day. Someone has said that the only thing we learn from history is that we do not learn. But we can learn, and one of our best approaches is through focusing our attention on intolerance and cruelty wherever they rear their ugly heads. The world is in a sorry condition today. Enslaved peoples with the courage to assert their freedom are being subjected for that reason alone to cruelty almost beyond the imagination of Americans. Our hearts go out to them and we pray for their delivery. We can do more. We can promote the cause of world brotherhood everywhere. First and most important, we can promote it here at home—in our states, in our cities, in our neighborhoods. The broader our base is here in America—the sounder our foundation—the more forceful our appeals can be in other parts of the world.

There is not a city in America but which could be bettered by a new or a strengthened unit of the National Conference of Christians and Jews. In these days when the development of the natural sciences is so greatly outstripping that of the social sciences, when such emphasis is being placed on the use of the natural sciences for aggressive war by some and for defense by others, it is more essential even than it was thirty years ago for men and women of good will in all faiths to join together for peace based upon brotherhood.

We are here for that purpose on Veterans Day, the day we celebrate not because of our victories, but to honor those faithful Americans who lost their lives fighting to protect our right to live in a world free from hatred, cruelty and aggression.

Surely it is a sufficiently high purpose for bringing together understanding people everywhere in the building of brotherhood, and for challenging their best efforts until justice, understanding and co-operation shall prevail as a way of life for the entire family of man.

Response to an Address by the Rt. Hon. Viscount Kilmuir, Lord High Chancellor of Great Britain, at the American Bar Association Convention in Westminster Hall

London, England, July 24, 1957

WE COME AS PILGRIMS to your beautiful land—not, however, as the Pilgrims of three and one half centuries ago came to our shores in search of a new home in a new land. We come as pilgrims to a shrine. With the blood of different races in our veins, and separated at home by distance as great as from our Atlantic shore to yours, but with one language and one concept of law, we make our pilgrimage to the land which gave both of those characteristics to our nation. Dedicated by birth to that language, and not only by birth but by profession to that concept of law, we come here in the spirit of brotherhood.

You are most generous to receive us, in this cordial manner, in historic Westminster Hall, where for so many centuries free institutions have been fashioned and the human values which we prize so highly have been preserved and kept adaptable to an ever changing world. It is with a feeling akin to reverence that we temporarily occupy the same seats which for ages have been used by those who hammered out the rights of mankind, as we conceive them to be, on the anvil of human experience.

Recently the second *Mayflower* made its colorful voyage to our shore. It has delighted us and stirred our historic interest. It was a splendid gesture of good will, and it is greatly appreciated. But it is the voyage of the first *Mayflower* that always thrills us. What a precious cargo it carried—102 men and women of religious faith, of resolute courage, and with the determination to make new homes in an unknown wilderness, under free institutions of their own making, in keeping with the dignity of Englishmen. As untutored as most of them were—and, being a minority group, as unaccustomed to governing as they were—even before they set foot on American soil they made the simple but solemn compact from which we trace that part of our constitutional system for which we claim credit. They covenanted to combine themselves together into "a civil body politic, for [their] better ordering and preservation," to enact "such just and equal laws . . . from time to time, as shall be thought most meet and convenient for the general good of the Colony" and under which they promised "all due submission and obedience."

We, in all parts of America, have tried to keep the faith with that compact. And except for the deviations occasioned by the frailty of human nature and the fallibility of the human mind, we have pursued a steady course to this day. It is still the core of the American's creed and our concept of "government of the people, by the people, [and] for the people."

Not the least precious part of the cargo brought by the Pilgrims on the first *Mayflower* was the common law. It certainly was the most enduring. They brought it, not in books, but in their minds, in the assumptions they carried with them regarding the rights of freeborn Englishmen. Modern scholarship has furnished increasing proof of the reception of the common law in the thirteen colonies. It was the common law in its most significant and vital aspect—not as a fixed body of rules, but as a mode of ascertaining and devising rules to meet the particular circumstances and changing conditions in which controversies and conflicts arise between man and man and man and government. That is the distinctive aspect of the common law; that is its glory. And I venture to believe it has been most strikingly and most fruitfully illustrated by what may be compendiously called the reception of the common law in the colonies and then, upon their gaining independence, in the states, and its prevalence in the United States today, barring only Louisiana. There, too, it has been infused into the basic law of the Code Napoleon, just as the common law has had its considerable influence upon the basic Dutch-Roman law of South Africa.

The hold of the common law in the United States is to be fairly deemed one of its most striking achievements because the adaptation that it has had to make in developing a new continent best proves the sturdiness of its roots. This early rooting of the common law in the United States was due in part to the very important influence exercised in the colonies by English-bred lawyers. They came to England from every colony, but particularly from the South, and were members of all of the four Inns. The habits of mind which they formed concerning the liberties and rights of the subject make it not surprising that among the leaders of the Revolution and the signers of the Declaration and the framers of the Constitution were these English-bred lawyers.

England as a training ground for Colonial lawyers was thus an important chapter in the unfolding of our law. Equal in importance, if not greater, must be deemed that classic of the common law, Blackstone's *Commentaries*. The story is old, but its meaning is permanent. The four volumes of the *Commentaries* were published in England between 1765 and 1769, and of these a thousand were imported into the colonies. Even more striking is the fact that for an American edition published in Philadelphia in 1771-1772, fifteen hundred sets were subscribed. Edmund Burke was well justified in telling the House of Commons, "In no country, perhaps, in the world is the law so general a study."

It is stating a fact and not boasting that, in all the countries where English is the tongue of the law, the common law has shown itself to be a process of constant rejuvenation to meet the demands of a progressive society, and particularly to make its adaptations to the new situations which our industrial civilization has thrown up. Our Law Reports and yours make manifest the interplay of influence between your courts and ours.

With you, as with us, however, lawmaking has for some time now ceased to be merely the law evolved by courts out of the principles of the common law. Long ago, the far-sighted Sir Henry Maine foresaw that legislation would become the greatest energy of lawmaking. This prophecy has been vindicated both in England and in the United States and, indeed, in all the English-speaking nations. In my Court, hardly a case arises in which legislation is not involved. But, even so, the methods of the common law are drawn upon—that is, the habits of mind with which, and the considerations by which, lawyers trained in the common law approach the judicial problems that legislation so often poses.

Insofar as the common law concerns the areas of judicial business which that phrase conventionally implies, I speak with a feeling of nostalgia. For the Court which I have the honor to represent has long ago ceased to be, within this narrow meaning, a common-law court. Its adjudications are now confined, broadly speaking, to questions arising under the United States Constitution and like problems of essentially national importance. The axis on which they turn is the nature of our legal system, and this is so very different from your own. You are spared the complexities of our federal system but are also denied the intellectual exactions which such a system makes upon lawyers.

But whether our concern is with a unitary system of government, like your own, or with a federalism such as those in Australia, Canada, India and the United States, a foundation of the common law has always been adequate for the maintenance of free institutions which meet the exactions of freedom-loving people. It has been adequate for us since the establishment of the first English colony in America.

Today, and for some months, in little Jamestown, Virginia, our people are celebrating the 350th anniversary of the establishment of that colony. Replicas of the three little ships which made that historic voyage ride at anchor in the James River. They represent much to us, and we celebrate the occasion not only as the first but as one of the most important milestones in our national history. In doing so, we express our great admiration for the things these founders brought with them—a belief in God, a love of freedom, and a concept of law upon which our free institutions have been built. This visit to you is but another manifestation of our lasting appreciation of that legacy.

III

The Scales of Justice

Supreme Court Decisions

Equality before the Law

Pete Hernandez v. State of Texas

347 US 475, 98 L ed 866, 74 S Ct 667

Decided May 3, 1954

In Jackson County, Texas, Pete Hernandez had been indicted for murder and convicted. The trial court rejected the
contention of defense counsel that American citizens of
Mexican descent were intentionally and systematically excluded from jury duty in Jackson County. On this ground,
defendant appealed to the Texas Court of Criminal Appeals.
This state court affirmed the conviction, ruling that the
Equal Protection Clause of the Fourteenth Amendment con-
templated only two classes, Negro and white.

Speaking for a unanimous Supreme Court, Chief Justice
Warren held that the conviction should be reversed because
the state court had erred in its limited interpretation of the
Fourteenth Amendment and because the case had established
that persons of Mexican descent had been denied equal protection under law.

THE PETITIONER, Pete Hernandez, was indicted for the murder of one Joe Espinosa by a grand jury in Jackson County,
Texas. He was convicted and sentenced to life imprisonment.

The Texas Court of Criminal Appeals affirmed the judgment of the trial court. —Tex Crim—, 251 SW2d 531. Prior to the trial, the petitioner, by his counsel, offered timely motions to quash the indictment and the jury panel. He alleged that persons of Mexican descent were systematically excluded from service as jury commissioners, grand jurors and petit jurors, although there were such persons fully qualified to serve residing in Jackson County. The petitioner asserted that exclusion of this class deprived him, as a member of the class, of the equal protection of the laws guaranteed by the Fourteenth Amendment of the Constitution. After a hearing, the trial court denied the motions. At the trial, the motions were renewed, further evidence taken, and the motions again denied. An allegation that the trial court erred in denying the motions was the sole basis of petitioner's appeal. In affirming the judgment of the trial court, the Texas Court of Criminal Appeals considered and passed upon the substantial Federal question raised by the petitioner. We granted a writ of certiorari to review that decision. 346 US 811, 98 L ed 339, 74 S Ct 52.

In numerous decisions, this Court has held that it is a denial of the equal protection of the laws to try a defendant of a particular race or color under an indictment issued by a grand jury, or before a petit jury, from which all persons of his race or color have, solely because of that race or color, been excluded by the State, whether acting through its legislature, its courts, or its executive or administrative officers. Although the Court has had little occasion to rule on the question directly, it has been recognized since Strauder v. West Virginia, 100 US 303, 25 L ed 664, that the exclusion of a class of persons from jury service on grounds other than race or color may also deprive a defendant who is a member of that class of the constitutional guarantee of equal protection of the laws. The State of Texas would have us hold that there are only two classes—white and Negro—within the contemplation of the Fourteenth Amendment. The decisions of this Court do not support that view. And, except where the question presented involves the exclusion of persons of Mexican descent from juries, Texas courts have taken a broader view of the scope of the equal-protection clause.

Throughout our history differences in race and color have defined easily identifiable groups which have at times required the aid of the courts in securing equal treatment under the laws. But community prejudices are not static, and from time to time other differences from the community norm may define other groups which need the same protection. Whether such a group exists within a community is a question of fact. When the existence of a distinct class is demonstrated, and it is further shown that the laws, as written or as applied, single out that class for different treatment not based on some reasonable classification, the guarantees of the Constitution have been violated. The Fourteenth Amendment is not directed solely against discrimination due to a "two-class theory"—that is, based upon differences between "white" and Negro.

As the petitioner acknowledges, the Texas system of selecting grand and petit jurors by the use of jury commissions is fair on its face and capable of being utilized without discrimination. But as this Court has held, the system is susceptible to abuse and can be employed in a discriminatory manner. The exclusion of otherwise eligible persons from jury service solely because of their ancestry or national origin is discrimination prohibited by the Fourteenth Amendment. The Texas statute makes no such discrimination, but the petitioner alleges that those administering the law do.

The petitioner's initial burden in substantiating his charge of group discrimination was to prove that persons of Mexican descent constitute a separate class in Jackson County, distinct from "whites." One method by which this may be demonstrated is by showing the attitude of the community. Here the testimony of responsible officials and citizens contained the admission that residents of the community distinguished between "white" and "Mexican." The participation of persons of Mexican descent in business and community groups was shown to be slight. Until very recent times, children of Mexican descent were required to attend a segregated school for the first four grades. At least one restaurant in town prominently displayed a sign announcing "No Mexicans Served." On the courthouse grounds at the time of the hearing, there were two men's toilets, one unmarked and the other marked "Colored Men" and "*Hombres Aqui*" (Men Here). No substantial evidence was offered to rebut the logical inference to be drawn from these facts, and it must be concluded that petitioner succeeded in his proof.

Having established the existence of a class, petitioner was then charged with the burden of proving discrimination. To do so, he relied on the pattern of proof established by Norris v. Alabama, 294 US 587, 79 L ed 1074, 55 S Ct 579. In that case, proof that Negroes constituted a substantial segment of the population of the jurisdiction, that some Negroes were qualified to serve as jurors, and that none had been called for jury service over an extended period of time was held to constitute prima-facie proof of the systematic exclusion of Negroes from jury service. This holding, sometimes called the "rule of exclusion," has been applied in other cases, and it is available in supplying proof of discrimination against any delineated class.

The petitioner established that 14 per cent of the population of Jackson County were persons with Mexican or Latin-American surnames, and that 11 per cent of the males over twenty-one bore such names. The County Tax Assessor testified that 6 or 7 per cent of the freeholders on the tax rolls of the county were persons of Mexican descent. The State of Texas stipulated that "for the last twenty-five years there is no record of any person with a Mexican or Latin-American name having served on a jury commission, grand jury or petit jury in Jackson County." The parties also stipulated that "there are some male persons of Mexican or Latin-American descent in Jackson County who, by virtue of being citizens, householders, or freeholders, and having all other legal prerequisites to jury service, are eligible to serve as members of a jury commission, grand jury and/or petit jury."

The petitioner met the burden of proof imposed in Norris v. Alabama (US) supra. To rebut the strong prima-facie case of the denial of the equal protection of the laws guaranteed by the Constitution thus established, the state offered the testimony of five jury commissioners that they had not discriminated against persons of Mexican or Latin-American descent in selecting jurors. They stated that their only objective had been to select those who they thought were best qualified. This testimony is not enough to overcome the petitioner's case. As the Court said in *Norris v. Alabama:*

That showing as to the long-continued exclusion of Negroes from jury service, and as to the many Negroes qualified for that service, could not be met by mere generalities. If, in the presence of such testimony as defendant adduced, the mere general assertions by officials of their performance of duty were to be accepted as an adequate justification for the complete exclusion of Negroes from jury service, the constitutional provision . . . would be but a vain and illusory requirement.

The same reasoning is applicable to these facts.

Circumstances or chance may well dictate that no persons in a certain class will serve on a particular jury or during some particular period. But it taxes our credulity to say that mere chance resulted in there being no members of this class among the over six thousand jurors called in the past twenty-five years. The result bespeaks discrimination, whether or not it was a conscious decision on the part of any individual jury commissioner. The judgment of conviction must be reversed.

To say that this decision revives the rejected contention that the Fourteenth Amendment requires proportional representation of all the component ethnic groups of the community on every jury ignores the facts. The petitioner did not seek proportional representation, nor did he claim a right to have persons of Mexican descent sit on the particular juries which he faced. His only claim is the right to be indicted and tried by juries from which all members of his class are not systematically excluded—juries selected from among all qualified persons regardless of national origin or descent. To this much, he is entitled by the Constitution.

Reversed.

Oliver Brown et al. v. Board of Educa-
tion of Topeka
347 US 483, 98 L ed 873, 74 S Ct 686

Decided May 17, 1954

In four different cases originating in as many states, Negro children had been denied admission to public schools attended by white children. In Kansas, plaintiffs were Negro children of elementary-school age who were refused admis-

sion to Topeka elementary schools under the provisions of a Kansas statute permitting cities of more than fifteen thousand population to maintain separate school facilities for Negroes and whites. In their case, Oliver Brown et al. v. Board of Education of Topeka, the United States District Court for the District of Kansas found that segregation in public education has a detrimental effect on Negro children. Nevertheless, the court declined to end segregation on the ground that the Kansas schools in question were substantially equal in facilities.

In South Carolina, plaintiffs were Negro children of elementary- and high-school age residing in Clarendon County who brought action to prohibit enforcement of state constitutional and statutory provisions requiring public-school segregation. In their case, Harry Briggs, Jr., et al. v. R. W. Elliott et al., the United States District Court for the Eastern District of South Carolina found that the Negro schools in Clarendon County were inferior to the white schools. The court ordered that equal facilities be provided for Negro schoolchildren, but it sustained the validity of state laws requiring segregation.

In a similar case in Virginia, Dorothy E. Davis et al. v. County School Board of Prince Edward County, plaintiffs were Negro children of high-school age residing in Prince Edward County who brought action to prohibit enforcement of state constitutional and statutory provisions requiring segregation in public schools. The United States District Court for the Eastern District of Virginia found, as did the Federal District Court in the South Carolina case, that the Negro schools in the county involved were inferior and ordered that equal facilities be provided. But, as in South Carolina, the state laws requiring segregation were upheld.

In Delaware, Negro children of elementary- and high-school age residing in New Castle County had brought action, Francis B. Gebhart et al. v. Ethel Louise Belton et al., to prohibit enforcement of state constitutional and statutory provisions requiring public-school segregation. Like the Federal District Courts in the South Carolina and Virginia cases, the Delaware Court of Chancery found that the Negro schools in question were inferior to the white schools. And, like the Federal District Court in the Kansas case, the Delaware court found that segregation in public education has a detrimental effect upon Negro children. The Delaware Court of Chancery ordered that the plaintiffs be immediately admitted to public schools previously attended only by white children, and this action was affirmed by the Supreme Court of Delaware.

The plaintiffs in the Kansas, South Carolina and Virginia cases appealed to the Supreme Court to void the various legal provisions in question which authorized and required racial segregation in public schools. Plaintiffs in these cases asked that the Supreme Court permit them to enter schools attended by white children in their respective districts. In the Delaware case, defendants appealed to the Supreme Court to reinstate segregation in the Delaware schools involved.

The Supreme Court grouped these four cases together under the heading of the Kansas case and ruled on all four simultaneously. In one of the most famous decisions ever handed down by the Supreme Court, Chief Justice Warren, speaking for a unanimous Court, held that separate educational facilities are inherently unequal, and that the "separate but equal" doctrine introduced in 1896 through the case Plessy v. Ferguson has no place in the field of public education.

The decision of the Supreme Court in Brown v. Board of Education held that the Equal Protection Clause of the Fourteenth Amendment prohibits the states from maintaining racially segregated schools and declared that opportunity

*for public education must be made available to all on equal
terms.*

THESE CASES come to us from the states of Kansas, South
Carolina, Virginia and Delaware. They are premised on different facts and different local conditions, but a common
legal question justifies their consideration together in this
consolidated opinion.

In each of the cases, minors of the Negro race, through
their legal representatives, seek the aid of the courts in obtaining admission to the public schools of their community
on a nonsegregated basis. In each instance, they had been
denied admission to schools attended by white children under laws requiring or permitting segregation according to
race. This segregation was alleged to deprive the plaintiffs
of the equal protection of the laws under the Fourteenth
Amendment. In each of the cases other than the Delaware
case, a three-judge Federal District Court denied relief to the
plaintiffs on the so-called "separate but equal" doctrine announced by this Court in Plessy v. Ferguson, 163 US 537, 41
L ed 256, 16 S Ct 1138. Under that doctrine, equality of
treatment is accorded when the races are provided substantially equal facilities, even though these facilities be separate.
In the Delaware case, the Supreme Court of Delaware adhered to that doctrine, but ordered that the plaintiffs be
admitted to the white schools because of their superiority
to the Negro schools.

The plaintiffs contend that segregated public schools are
not "equal" and cannot be made "equal," and that hence
they are deprived of the equal protection of the laws. Because of the obvious importance of the question presented,
the Court took jurisdiction. Argument was heard in the 1952

Term, and reargument was heard this Term on certain questions propounded by the Court.

Reargument was largely devoted to the circumstances surrounding the adoption of the Fourteenth Amendment in 1868. It covered exhaustively consideration of the Amendment in Congress, ratification by the states, then-existing practices in racial segregation, and the views of proponents and opponents of the Amendment. This discussion and our own investigation convince us that, although these sources cast some light, it is not enough to resolve the problem with which we are faced. At best, they are inconclusive. The most avid proponents of the postwar Amendments undoubtedly intended them to remove all legal distinctions among "all persons born or naturalized in the United States." Their opponents, just as certainly, were antagonistic to both the letter and the spirit of the Amendments and wished them to have the most limited effect. What others in Congress and the state legislatures had in mind cannot be determined with any degree of certainty.

An additional reason for the inconclusive nature of the Amendment's history, with respect to segregated schools, is the status of public education at that time. In the South, the movement toward free common schools, supported by general taxation, had not yet taken hold. Education of white children was largely in the hands of private groups. Education of Negroes was almost nonexistent, and practically all of the race were illiterate. In fact, any education of Negroes was forbidden by law in some states. Today, in contrast, many Negroes have achieved outstanding success in the arts and sciences as well as in the business and professional world. It is true that public-school education at the time of the Amendment had advanced further in the North, but the effect of the Amendment on Northern states was generally ignored in the Congressional debates. Even in the North, the conditions of public education did not approximate those existing today. The curriculum was usually rudimentary; ungraded schools were common in rural areas; the school term was but three months a year in many states; and compulsory school attendance was virtually unknown. As a consequence, it is not surprising that there should be so little in the history of the Fourteenth Amendment relating to its intended effect on public education.

In the first cases in this Court construing the Fourteenth Amendment, decided shortly after its adoption, the Court interpreted it as proscribing all state-imposed discriminations against the Negro race. The doctrine of "separate but equal" did not make its appearance in this Court until 1896 in the case of Plessy v. Ferguson (US) supra, involving not education but transportation. American courts have since labored with the doctrine for over half a century. In this Court, there have been six cases involving the "separate but equal" doctrine in the field of public education. In Cumming v. County Board of Education, 175 US 528, 44 L ed 262, 20 S Ct 197, and Gong Lum v. Rice, 275 US 78, 72 L ed 172, 48 S Ct 91, the validity of the doctrine itself was not challenged. In more recent cases, all on the graduate-school level, inequality was found in that specific benefits enjoyed by white students were denied to Negro students of the same educational qualifications. Missouri ex rel. Gaines v. Canada, 305 US 337, 83 L ed 208, 59 S Ct 232; Sipuel v. University of Oklahoma, 332 US 631, 92 L ed 247, 68 S Ct 299; Sweatt v. Painter, 339 US 629, 94 L ed 1114, 70 S Ct 848; McLaurin v. Oklahoma State Regents, 339 US 637, 94 L ed 1149, 70 S Ct 851. In none of these cases was it necessary to re-examine the doctrine to grant relief to the Negro plaintiff. And in Sweatt v. Painter (US) supra, the Court expressly reserved decision on the question whether Plessy v. Ferguson should be held inapplicable to public education.

In the instant cases, that question is directly presented. Here, unlike *Sweatt v. Painter*, there are findings below that the Negro and white schools involved have been equalized, or are being equalized, with respect to buildings, curricula, qualifications and salaries of teachers, and other "tangible" factors. Our decision, therefore, cannot turn on merely a comparison of these tangible factors in the Negro and white schools involved in each of the cases. We must look instead to the effect of segregation itself on public education.

In approaching this problem, we cannot turn the clock back to 1868 when the Amendment was adopted, or even to 1896 when *Plessy v. Ferguson* was written. We must consider public education in the light of its full development and its present place in American life throughout the nation. Only in this way can it be determined if segregation in public schools deprives these plaintiffs of the equal protection of the laws.

Today, education is perhaps the most important function of state and local governments. Compulsory school attendance laws and the great expenditures for education both demonstrate our recognition of the importance of education to our democratic society. It is required in the performance of our most basic public responsibilities, even service in the armed forces. It is the very foundation of good citizenship. Today it is a principal instrument in awakening the child to cultural values, in preparing him for later professional training, and in helping him to adjust normally to his environment. In these days, it is doubtful that any child may reasonably be expected to succeed in life if he is denied the opportunity of an education. Such an opportunity, where the state has undertaken to provide it, is a right which must be made available to all on equal terms.

We come then to the question presented: Does segregation of children in public schools solely on the basis of race, even though the physical facilities and other "tangible" factors may be equal, deprive the children of the minority group of equal educational opportunities? We believe that it does.

In Sweatt v. Painter (US) supra, in finding that a segregated law school for Negroes could not provide them equal educational opportunities, this Court relied in large part on "those qualities which are incapable of objective measurement but which make for greatness in a law school." In McLaurin v. Oklahoma State Regents, 339 US 637, 94 L ed 1149, 70 S Ct 851, supra, the Court, in requiring that a Negro admitted to a white graduate school be treated like all other students, again resorted to intangible considerations: ". . . his ability to study, to engage in discussions and exchange views with other students, and, in general, to learn his profession." Such considerations apply with added force to children in grade and high schools. To separate them from others of similar age and qualifications solely because of their race generates a feeling of inferiority as to their status in the community that may affect their hearts and minds in a way unlikely ever to be undone. The effect of this separation on their educational opportunities was well stated by a finding in the Kansas case by a court which nevertheless felt compelled to rule against the Negro plaintiffs:

Segregation of white and colored children in public schools has a detrimental effect upon the colored children. The impact is greater when it has the sanction of the law; for the policy of separating the races is usually interpreted as denoting the inferiority of the Negro group. A sense of inferiority affects the motivation of a child to learn. Segregation with the sanction of law, therefore, has a tendency to [retard] the educational and mental development of Negro children and to deprive them of some of the benefits they would receive in a racial[ly] integrated school system.

Whatever may have been the extent of psychological knowledge at the time of *Plessy v. Ferguson*, this finding is amply supported by modern authority. Any language in *Plessy v. Ferguson* contrary to this finding is rejected.

We conclude that in the field of public education the doctrine of "separate but equal" has no place. Separate educational facilities are inherently unequal. Therefore, we hold that the plaintiffs and others similarly situated for whom the actions have been brought are, by reason of the segregation complained of, deprived of the equal protection of the laws guaranteed by the Fourteenth Amendment. This disposition makes unnecessary any discussion whether such segregation also violates the Due Process Clause of the Fourteenth Amendment.

Because these are class actions, because of the wide applicability of this decision, and because of the great variety of local conditions, the formulation of decrees in these cases presents problems of considerable complexity. On reargument, the consideration of appropriate relief was necessarily subordinated to the primary question—the constitutionality of segregation in public education. We have now announced that such segregation is a denial of the equal protection of the laws. In order that we may have the full assistance of the parties in formulating decrees, the cases will be restored to the docket, and the parties are requested to present further argument on Questions 4 and 5 previously propounded by the Court for the reargument this Term. The Attorney General of the United States is again invited to participate. The Attorneys General of the states requiring or permitting segregation in public education will also be permitted to appear as *amici curiae* upon request to do so by September 15, 1954, and submission of briefs by October 1, 1954.

It is so ordered.

Spottswood Thomas Bolling et al. v. C.
Melvin Sharpe et al.

347 US 497, 98 L ed 884, 74 S Ct 693

Decided May 17, 1954

The Supreme Court, in the Brown v. Board of Education
decision written by Chief Justice Warren, unanimously held
that the Equal Protection Clause of the Fourteenth Amendment prohibits the states from maintaining racially segregated schools. In this companion case, petitioners were also
Negro children, in this instance seeking admission to the
segregated public schools of the District of Columbia. Again
speaking for a unanimous Court, Chief Justice Warren held
that racial segregation in the public schools of the District
of Columbia denied due process of law as guaranteed by the
Fifth Amendment.

THIS CASE challenges the validity of segregation in the public
schools of the District of Columbia. The petitioners, minors
of the Negro race, allege that such segregation deprives them
of due process of law under the Fifth Amendment. They
were refused admission to a public school attended by white
children solely because of their race. They sought the aid of
the District Court for the District of Columbia in obtaining
admission. That Court dismissed their complaint. The Court

granted a writ of certiorari before judgment in the Court of Appeals because of the importance of the constitutional question presented. 344 US 873, 97 L ed 676, 73 S Ct 173.

We have this day held that the Equal Protection Clause of the Fourteenth Amendment prohibits the states from maintaining racially segregated public schools. The legal problem in the District of Columbia is somewhat different, however. The Fifth Amendment, which is applicable in the District of Columbia, does not contain an equal-protection clause as does the Fourteenth Amendment, which applies only to the states. But the concepts of equal protection and due process, both stemming from our American ideal of fairness, are not mutually exclusive. The "equal protection of the laws" is a more explicit safeguard of prohibited unfairness than "due process of law," and, therefore, we do not imply that the two are always interchangeable phrases. But, as this Court has recognized, discrimination may be so unjustifiable as to be violative of due process.

Classifications based solely upon race must be scrutinized with particular care, since they are contrary to our traditions and hence constitutionally suspect. As long ago as 1896, this Court declared the principle "that the Constitution of the United States, in its present form, forbids, so far as civil and political rights are concerned, discrimination by the General Government, or by the States, against any citizen because of his race." And in Buchanan v. Warley, 245 US 60, 62 L ed 149, 38 S Ct 16, LRA1918C 210, Ann Cas 1918A 1201, the Court held that a statute which limited the right of a property owner to convey his property to a person of another race was, as an unreasonable discrimination, a denial of due process of law.

Although the Court has not assumed to define "liberty" with any great precision, that term is not confined to mere freedom from bodily restraint. Liberty under law extends to the full range of conduct which the individual is free to pursue, and it cannot be restricted except for a proper governmental objective. Segregation in public education is not reasonably related to any proper governmental objective, and thus it imposes on Negro children of the District of Columbia a burden that constitutes an arbitrary deprivation of their liberty in violation of the Due Process Clause.

In view of our decision that the Constitution prohibits the states from maintaining racially segregated public schools, it would be unthinkable that the same Constitution would impose a lesser duty on the Federal Government. We hold that racial segregation in the public schools of the District of Columbia is a denial of the due process of law guaranteed by the Fifth Amendment to the Constitution.

For the reasons set out in *Brown v. Board of Education*, this case will be restored to the docket for reargument on Questions 4 and 5 previously propounded by the Court. 345 US 972, 97 L ed 1388, 73 S Ct 1174.

It is so ordered.

Oliver Brown et al. v. Board of Education of Topeka
349 US 294, 99 L ed 1083, 75 S Ct 753

Decided May 31, 1955

In the case of Brown v. Board of Education, from Kansas, and the three companion cases from South Carolina, Virginia and Delaware, the Supreme Court unanimously held that the practice of maintaining racially segregated public schools in any state was unconstitutional. And in the case of Bolling v. Sharpe, the Court unanimously held that the practice of maintaining racially segregated public schools in the District of Columbia was likewise unconstitutional.

These cases were decided on May 17, 1954, and one year later, on May 31, 1955, Chief Justice Warren delivered a supplementary decision on behalf of a unanimous Court. The supplementary decision directed that lower courts were to retain jurisdiction in all cases involving racially segregated public schools, and that these courts were to apply the appropriate rulings set forth in Brown v. Board of Education and Bolling v. Sharpe.

This supplementary decision established the principle that defendants in such cases should make a prompt and reasonable start toward compliance with the decision requiring desegregation, and when defendants requested delay, the burden of proof rested upon them to establish the need for such delay.

THESE CASES were decided on May 17, 1954. The opinions of that date, declaring the fundamental principle that racial discrimination in public education is unconstitutional, are incorporated herein by reference. All provisions of Federal, state, or local law requiring or permitting such discrimination must yield to this principle. There remains for consideration the manner in which relief is to be accorded.

Because these cases arose under different local conditions and their disposition will involve a variety of local problems, we requested further argument on the question of relief. In view of the nationwide importance of the decision, we invited the Attorney General of the United States and the Attorneys General of all states requiring or permitting racial discrimination in public education to present their views on that question. The parties, the United States, and the States of Florida, North Carolina, Arkansas, Oklahoma, Maryland and Texas filed briefs and participated in the oral argument.

These presentations were informative and helpful to the Court in its consideration of the complexities arising from the transition to a system of public education freed of racial discrimination. The presentations also demonstrated that substantial steps to eliminate racial discrimination in public schools have already been taken, not only in some of the communities in which these cases arose, but in some states appearing as *amici curiae*, and in other states as well. Substantial progress has been made in the District of Columbia and in the communities in Kansas and Delaware involved in this litigation. The defendants in the cases coming to us from South Carolina and Virginia are awaiting the decision of this Court concerning relief.

Full implementation of these constitutional principles may require solution of varied local school problems. School authorities have the primary responsibility for elucidating, assessing and solving these problems; courts will have to consider whether the action of school authorities constitutes good-faith implementation of the governing constitutional principles. Because of their proximity to local conditions and the possible need for further hearings, the courts which originally heard these cases can best perform this judicial appraisal. Accordingly, we believe it appropriate to remand the cases to those courts.

In fashioning and effectuating the decrees, the courts will be guided by equitable principles. Traditionally, equity has been characterized by a practical flexibility in shaping its remedies and by a facility for adjusting and reconciling public and private needs. These cases call for the exercise of these traditional attributes of equity power. At stake is the personal interest of the plaintiffs in admission to public schools as soon as practicable on a nondiscriminatory basis. To effectuate this interest may call for elimination of a variety of obstacles in making the transition to school systems operated in accordance with the constitutional principles set forth in our May 17, 1954, decision. Courts of equity may properly take into account the public interest in the elimination of such obstacles in a systematic and effective manner. But it should go without saying that the vitality of these constitutional principles cannot be allowed to yield simply because of disagreement with them.

While giving weight to these public and private considerations, the courts will require that the defendants make a prompt and reasonable start toward full compliance with our May 17, 1954, ruling. Once such a start has been made, the courts may find that additional time is necessary to carry out the ruling in an effective manner. The burden rests upon the defendants to establish that such time is necessary in the public interest and is consistent with good-faith compliance at the earliest practicable date. To that end, the courts may consider problems related to administration, arising from the physical condition of the school plant, the school transportation system, personnel, revision of school districts and attendance areas into compact units to achieve a system of determining admission to the public schools on a non-racial basis, and revision of local laws and regulations which may be necessary in solving the foregoing problems. They will also consider the adequacy of any plans the defendants may propose to meet these problems and to effectuate a transition to a racially nondiscriminatory school system. During this period of transition, the courts will retain jurisdiction of these cases.

The judgments below, except that in the Delaware case,

are accordingly reversed and the cases are remanded to the District Courts to take such proceedings and enter such orders and decrees consistent with this opinion as are necessary and proper to admit to public schools on a racially nondiscriminatory basis with all deliberate speed the parties to these cases. The judgment in the Delaware case—ordering the immediate admission of the plaintiffs to schools previously attended only by white children—is affirmed on the basis of the principles stated in our May 17, 1954, opinion, but the case is remanded to the Supreme Court of Delaware for such further proceedings as that court may deem necessary in light of this opinion.

It is so ordered.

Justice under Law

Commonwealth of Pennsylvania v.
Steve Nelson
350 US 497, 100 L ed 640, 76 S Ct 477

Decided May 14, 1956

Steve Nelson, charged with violating the Pennsylvania Sedition Act, was convicted in the Court of Quarter Sessions of Allegheny County, Pennsylvania, and his conviction was affirmed by the Superior Court. The Supreme Court of Pennsylvania set aside the conviction.

The question considered by the United States Supreme Court was whether the Federal Smith Act, which prohibits advocacy of the overthrow of the United States Government by force or violence, supersedes state legislation such as the Pennsylvania Sedition Act. Chief Justice Warren was joined by Justices Black, Frankfurter, Douglas, Clark and Harlan in holding that the dominant Federal interest in this field precludes state intervention and that administration of such *state acts would conflict with enforcement of Federal law. Justice Reed, joined by Justices Burton and Minton, dissented.*

THE RESPONDENT Steve Nelson, an acknowledged member of the Communist Party, was convicted in the Court of Quarter Sessions of Allegheny County, Pennsylvania, of a violation of the Pennsylvania Sedition Act and sentenced to imprisonment for twenty years and to a fine of $10,000 and to costs of prosecution in the sum of $13,000. The Superior Court affirmed the conviction. 172 Pa Super 125, 92 A2d 431. The Supreme Court of Pennsylvania, recognizing but not reaching many alleged serious trial errors and conduct of the trial court infringing upon respondent's right to due process of law, decided the case on the narrow issue of supersession of the state law by the Federal Smith Act. In its opinion, the court stated:

And, while the Pennsylvania statute proscribes sedition against either the Government of the United States or the Government of Pennsylvania, it is only alleged sedition against the United States with which the instant case is concerned. Out of all the voluminous testimony, we have not found, nor has anyone pointed to, a single word indicating a seditious act or even utterance directed against the Government of Pennsylvania.

The precise holding of the court, and all that is before us for review, is that the Smith Act of 1940, as amended in 1948, which prohibits the knowing advocacy of the overthrow of the Government of the United States by force and violence, supersedes the enforceability of the Pennsylvania Sedition Act which proscribes the same conduct.

Many state Attorneys General and the Solicitor General of the United States appeared as *amici curiae* for petitioner, and several briefs were filed on behalf of the respondent. Because of the important question of Federal-state relationship, we granted certiorari. 348 US 814, 99 L ed 642, 75 S Ct 58.

It should be said at the outset that the decision in this case does not affect the right of states to enforce their sedition laws at times when the Federal Government has not occupied the field and is not protecting the entire country from seditious conduct. The distinction between the two situations was clearly recognized by the court below. Nor does it limit the jurisdiction of the states where the Constitution and Congress have specifically given them concurrent jurisdiction, as was done under the Eighteenth Amendment and the Volstead Act. United States v. Lanza, 260 US 377, 67 L ed 314, 43 S Ct 141. Neither does it limit the right of the state to protect itself at any time against sabotage or attempted violence of all kinds. Nor does it prevent the state from prosecuting where the same act constitutes both a Federal offense and a state offense under the police power, as was done in Fox v. Ohio (US) 5 How 410, 12 L ed 213, and Gilbert v. Minnesota, 254 US 325, 65 L ed 287, 41 S Ct 125, relied upon by petitioner as authority herein. In neither of those cases did the state statute impinge on Federal jurisdiction. In the Fox case the Federal offense was counterfeiting. The state offense was defrauding the person to whom the spurious money was passed. In the Gilbert case this Court, in upholding the enforcement of a state statute proscribing conduct which would "interfere with or discourage the enlistment of men in the military or naval forces of the United States or of the State of Minnesota," treated it not as an act relating to "the raising of armies for the national defense, nor to rules and regulations for the government of those under arms [a constitutionally exclusive Federal power]. It [was] simply a local police measure. . . ."

Where, as in the instant case, Congress has not stated specifically whether a Federal statute has occupied a field in which the states are otherwise free to legislate, different criteria have furnished touchstones for decision. Thus,

[this] Court, in considering the validity of state laws in the light of . . . Federal laws touching the same subject, has made use of the following expressions: conflicting; contrary to; occupying the field; repugnance; difference; irreconcilability; inconsistency; violation; curtailment; and interference. But none of these expressions provides an infallible constitutional test or an exclusive constitutional yardstick. In the final analysis, there can be no one crystal clear distinctly marked formula. [Hines v. Davidowitz, 312 US 52, 67, 85 L ed 581, 586, 61 S Ct 399.]

And see Rice v. Santa Fe Elevator Corp., 331 US 218, 230, 231, 91 L ed 1447, 1459, 1460, 67 S Ct 1146. In this case, we think that each of several tests of supersession is met.

First, "[the] scheme of federal regulation [is] so pervasive as to make reasonable the inference that Congress left no room for the States to supplement it." Rice v. Santa Fe Elevator Corp., 331 US at 230. The Congress determined in 1940 that it was necessary for it to re-enter the field of antisubversive legislation, which had been abandoned by it in 1921. In that year, it enacted the Smith Act, which proscribes advocacy of the overthrow of any government—Federal, state or local—by force and violence, and organization of and knowing membership in a group which so advocates. Conspiracy to commit any of these acts is punishable under the general criminal-conspiracy provisions in 18 USC § 371. The Internal Security Act of 1950 is aimed more directly at Communist organizations. It distinguishes between "Communist-action organizations" and "Communist-front organizations," requiring such organizations to register and to file annual reports with the Attorney General giving complete details as to their officers and funds. Members of Communist-action organizations who have not been registered by their organization must register as individuals. Failure to register in accordance with the requirements of §§ 786-787 is punishable by a fine of not more than $10,000 for an offending organization and by a fine of not more than $10,000 or imprisonment for not more than five years or both for an individual offender—each day of failure to register constituting a separate offense. And the act imposes certain sanctions upon both "action" and "front" organizations and their members. The Communist Control Act of 1954 declares that "the Communist Party of the United States, although purportedly a political party, is in fact an instrumentality of a conspiracy to overthrow the Government of the United States" and that "its role as the agency of a hostile foreign power renders its existence a clear present and continuing danger to the security of the United States." It also contains a legislative finding that the Communist Party is a "Communist-action organization" within the meaning of the Internal Security Act of 1950 and provides that "knowing" members of the Communist Party are "subject to all the provisions and penalties" of that act. It furthermore sets up a new classification of "Communist-infiltrated organizations" and provides for the imposition of sanctions against them.

We examine these acts only to determine the Congressional plan. Looking to all of them in the aggregate, the conclusion is inescapable that Congress has intended to occupy the field of sedition. Taken as a whole, they evince a Congressional plan which makes it reasonable to determine that no room has been left for the states to supplement it. Therefore, a state sedition statute is superseded regardless of whether it purports to supplement the Federal law. As was said by Mr. Justice Holmes in Charleston & W.C.R. Co. v. Varnville Furniture Co., 237 US 597, 604, 59 L ed 1137, 1140, 35 S Ct 715, Ann Cas 1916D 333:

"When Congress has taken the particular subject matter in hand coincidence is as ineffective as opposition, and a state law is not to be declared a help because it attempts to go farther than Congress has seen fit to go."

Second, the Federal statutes "touch a field in which the federal interest is so dominant that the federal system [must] be assumed to preclude enforcement of state laws on the same subject." Rice v. Santa Fe Elevator Corp., 331 US at 230, citing Hines v. Davidowitz, 312 US 52, 85 L ed 581, 61 S Ct 399, *supra*. Congress has devised an all-embracing program for resistance to the various forms of totalitarian aggression. Our external defenses have been strengthened, and a plan to protect against internal subversion has been made by it. It has appropriated vast sums, not only for our own protection, but also to strengthen freedom throughout the world. It has charged the Federal Bureau of Investigation and the Central Intelligence Agency with responsibility for intelligence concerning Communist seditious activities against our government, and has denominated such activities as part of a world conspiracy. It accordingly proscribed sedition against all government in the nation—national, state and local. Congress declared that these steps were taken "to provide for the common defense, to preserve the sovereignty of the United States as an independent nation, and to guarantee to each State a republican form of government. . . ." Congress having thus treated seditious conduct as a matter of vital national concern, it is in no sense a local enforcement problem. As was said in the court below:

Sedition against the United States is not a local offense. It is a crime against the Nation. As such, it should be prosecuted and punished in the Federal courts where this defendant has in fact been prosecuted and convicted and is now under sentence. It is not only important but vital that such prosecutions should be exclusively within the control of the Federal Government. . . .

Third, enforcement of state sedition acts presents a serious danger of conflict with the administration of the Federal program. Since 1939, in order to avoid a hampering of uniform enforcement of its program by sporadic local prosecutions, the Federal Government has urged local authorities not to intervene in such matters, but to turn over to the Federal authorities immediately and unevaluated all information concerning subversive activities. The President made such a request on September 6, 1939, when he placed the Federal Bureau of Investigation in charge of investigation in this field:

The Attorney General has been requested by me to instruct the Federal Bureau of Investigation of the Department of Justice to take charge of investigative work in matters relating to espionage, sabotage, and violations of the neutrality regulations.

This task must be conducted in a comprehensive and effective manner on a national basis, and all information must be carefully sifted out and correlated in order to avoid confusion and irresponsibility.

To this end I request all police officers, sheriffs, and all other law enforcement officers in the United States promptly to turn over to the nearest representative of the Federal

Bureau of Investigation any information obtained by them relating to espionage, counterespionage, sabotage, subversive activities and violations of the neutrality laws.

And in addressing the Federal-State Conference on Law Enforcement Problems of National Defense, held on August 5 and 6, 1940, only a few weeks after the passage of the Smith Act, the Director of the Federal Bureau of Investigation said:

The fact must not be overlooked that meeting the spy, the saboteur and the subverter is a problem that must be handled on a nation-wide basis. An isolated incident in the middle west may be of little significance, but when fitted into a national pattern of similar incidents, it may lead to an important revelation of subversive activity. It is for this reason that the President requested all of our citizens and law enforcing agencies to report directly to the Federal Bureau of Investigation any complaints or information dealing with espionage, sabotage or subversive activities. In such matters, time is of the essence. It is unfortunate that in a few States efforts have been made by individuals not fully acquainted with the far-flung ramifications of this problem to interject superstructures of agencies between local law enforcement and the FBI to sift what might be vital information, thus delaying its immediate reference to the FBI. This cannot be, if our internal security is to be best served. This is no time for red tape or amateur handling of such vital matters. There must be a direct and free flow of contact between the local law enforcement agencies and the FBI. The job of meeting the spy or saboteur is one for experienced men of law enforcement.

Moreover, the Pennsylvania statute presents a peculiar danger of interference with the Federal program. For, as the court below observed:

Unlike the Smith Act, which can be administered only by Federal officers acting in their official capacities, indictment for sedition under the Pennsylvania statute can be initiated upon an information made by a private individual. The opportunity thus present for the indulgence of personal spite and hatred or for furthering some selfish advantage or ambition need only be mentioned to be appreciated. Defense of the Nation by law, no less than by arms, should be a public and not a private undertaking. It is important that punitive sanctions for sedition against the United States be such as have been promulgated by the central governmental authority and administered under the supervision and review of that authority's judiciary. If that be done, sedition will be detected and punished, no less, wherever it may be found, and the right of the individual to speak freely and without fear, even in criticism of the government, will at the same time be protected.

In his brief, the Solicitor General states that forty-two states plus Alaska and Hawaii have statutes which in some form prohibit advocacy of the violent overthrow of established government. These statutes are entitled antisedition statutes, criminal-anarchy laws, criminal-syndicalist laws, etc. Although all of them are primarily directed against the overthrow of the United States Government, they are in no sense uniform. And our attention has not been called to any case where the prosecution has been successfully directed against an attempt to destroy state or local government. Some of these acts are studiously drawn and purport to protect fundamental rights by appropriate definitions, standards of proof and orderly procedures in keeping with the avowed Congressional purpose "to protect freedom from those who would destroy it, without infringing upon the freedom of all our people." Others are vague and are almost wholly without such safeguards. Some even purport to punish mere membership in subversive organizations which the Federal statutes do not punish where Federal registration requirements have been fulfilled.

When we were confronted with a like situation in the field of labor-management relations, Mr. Justice Jackson wrote:

"A multiplicity of tribunals and a diversity of procedures are quite as apt to produce incompatible or conflicting adjudications as are different rules of substantive law."

Should the states be permitted to exercise a concurrent jurisdiction in this area, Federal enforcement would encounter not only the difficulties mentioned by Mr. Justice Jackson, but the added conflict engendered by different criteria of substantive offenses.

Since we find that Congress has occupied the field to the exclusion of parallel state legislation, that the dominant interest of the Federal Government precludes state intervention, and that administration of state acts would conflict with the operation of the Federal plan, we are convinced that the decision of the Supreme Court of Pennsylvania is unassailable.

We are not unmindful of the risk of compounding punishments which would be created by finding concurrent state power. In our view of the case, we do not reach the question whether double or multiple punishment for the same overt acts directed against the United States has constitutional sanction. Without compelling indication to the contrary, we will not assume that Congress intended to permit the possibility of double punishment. Cf. Houston v. Moore (US) 5 Wheat 1, 31, 75, 5 L ed 19, 26, 37; Jerome v. United States, 318 US 101, 105, 87 L ed 640, 643, 63 S Ct 483.

The judgment of the Supreme Court of Pennsylvania is Affirmed.

Stephen Mesarosh, also known as
Steve Nelson, et al. v. United States
of America
352 US 1, 1 L ed 2d 1, 77 S Ct 1

Decided November 5, 1956

In an earlier case, Pennsylvania v. Nelson, decided on May
14, 1956, the Supreme Court reviewed the conviction of
Steve Nelson under the Pennsylvania Sedition Act. In this
entirely separate case, the Court reviewed his conviction and
that of his associates under Federal legislation in the field of
sedition. They were convicted in the United States District
Court for the Western District of Pennsylvania for violating
the Smith Act by conspiring to advocate the overthrow of
the United States Government by force and violence. Their
conviction was affirmed by the United States Court of Appeals for the Third Circuit. Because a Government witness
in the case had given untruthful testimony in other similar
trials, the Solicitor General of the United States did not ask
that the convictions be affirmed, but instead asked that the
case be remanded to the trial court to determine whether a
new trial should be held.

Chief Justice Warren was joined by Justices Black, Reed,
Douglas and Clark in holding that the convictions should be
reversed and a wholly new trial should be held. Justice Har-

lan, joined by Justices Frankfurter and Burton, dissented, declaring that the case should be remanded to the trial court. Justice Brennan did not participate in the case.

THE DECISION herein passes only on the integrity of a criminal trial in the Federal courts. It does not determine the guilt or innocence of the petitioners, and we do not reach other issues propounded in the lengthy briefs or which may be present in the trial record of 5,147 pages. The Solicitor General of the United States moved to remand the case to the trial court for further proceedings because of untruthful testimony given before other tribunals by Joseph D. Mazzei, a Government witness in this case. The countermotion of petitioners asked for a new trial. The decision is based entirely upon the representations of the Government in its written motion and on the statements of the Solicitor General during the argument on the motions.

The petitioners were charged in a one-count indictment in the District Court for the Western District of Pennsylvania with conspiracy to violate the Smith Act. They were convicted, and the Court of Appeals for the Third Circuit, sitting en banc, affirmed by a divided court. 223 F 2d 449. This Court granted the petition for writ of certiorari, 350 US 922, 100 L ed 807, 76 S Ct 218, and the case was scheduled for argument on October 10, 1956.

On September 27, 1956, the Solicitor General of the United States filed a motion calling the attention of the Court to the testimony given in other proceedings by Mazzei, who was one of the seven witnesses for the Government in this case. In his motion, he stated that the Government, on the information in its possession, now has serious reason to doubt the truthfulness of Mazzei's testimony in those proceedings. While adhering to its position that "the testimony given by Mazzei at the trial [in this case] was entirely truthful and credible," the motion stated that "these incidents, taken cumulatively, lead us to suggest that the issue of his truthfulness at the trial of these petitioners should now be determined by the District Court after a hearing."

The material cited by the Government indicating the untruthfulness of Mazzei on occasions other than this trial can best be presented by setting forth verbatim the description of these incidents presented in the Motion of the Government to Remand:

On June 18, 1953, Mazzei testified before the Senate Permanent Subcommittee on Investigations, in Washington, D.C., that, at a meeting of the Civil Rights Congress on December 4, 1952, one Louis Bortz told him that he, Bortz, had been "selected by the Communist Party to do a job in the liquidation of Senator Joseph McCarthy." Mazzei further testified that the said Bortz conducted Communist Party classes in Pittsburgh to familiarize Party members with the handling of firearms and to instruct them in the construction of bombs.

On November 14, 1952, Mazzei pleaded guilty to charges of adultery and bastardy in a Pennsylvania state court. This fact was brought out during his cross-examination at the petitioners' trial. On October 2, 1953—after the completion of the trial—Mazzei filed a petition in the state court to have the guilty plea set aside. One of the grounds set forth in his petition was that he "was not guilty of the charge to which he was induced to plead . . . but did so only in his official capacity [as a Government informant] at the insistence of his superior in the FBI to avoid testifying." At a hearing on the above petition on October 6, 1953, a Special Agent of the FBI denied Mazzei's allegations under oath. Mazzei's petition was dismissed by the Court on October 6, 1953.

In November 1953, Mazzei, at a secret proceeding, identified a certain Government official as a long-time active Communist Party member.

On June 10 and 11, 1955, Mazzei testified before the Senate Subcommittee on Internal Security regarding possible Communist influences motivating attempts to discredit Justice Michael Musmanno of the Supreme Court of Pennsylvania. In the course of his testimony, Mazzei identified John J. Mullen, National Director, Political Action Committee, Steel Workers of America, as a member of the Communist Party in Pittsburgh during the period that Mazzei was a Government informant. Mazzei also testified that since 1942 he met Mullen ten or fifteen times a year, as a fellow Communist Party member.

On July 2, 1956, Mazzei testified in disbarment proceedings against one Leo Sheiner before the Circuit Court of the Eleventh Judicial Circuit of Florida, in Miami. On cross-examination, Mazzei reiterated his charge that he was induced to plead guilty to the adultery and bastardy charge in the Pennsylvania state court in November 1952 by an agent of the FBI. Items of his testimony as to alleged Communist activity are as follows: that he visited Dade County, Florida, on behalf of the Communist Party during each of the years from 1946 to 1952; that the Communist Party in Miami had attempted to lease a bus line which served the Opa-locka Air Base; that in 1948 the Communist Party made plans for the armed invasion of the United States on orders from the Soviet Union and that he, Mazzei, was selected to go to Miami in 1948 because it was a seaport; that he took courses in the Communist Party on sabotage, espionage, and handling arms and ammunition; that he was taught by officers of the Communist Party in Pittsburgh how to blow bridges, poison water in reservoirs, and to eliminate people; that he discussed with Sheiner in 1948 "knocking off" a Judge Holt (a Florida judge) whom they (presumably the Communist Party) were having trouble with, and importing one Louis Bortz, the strong-arm man for the Communist Party, to do the job; that he and the Communist Party had made plans to assassinate Senators, Congressmen, and even went to Washington and beat up a Senator; and that, to his knowledge, Sheiner was extensively engaged in Communist Party activities in 1945, 1947, 1950, 1951 and 1952. None of this testimony at the Florida proceeding is supported or corroborated by information in the possession of the Government.

Mazzei likewise testified that the FBI arranged to get him into the Army so that he could watch a certain Communist Party member; that he never wore a uniform and that he was discharged the day after the Communist Party member he was to watch was discharged. In actual fact, Mazzei's career in the Army was the result of the operation of the Selective Training and Service Act of 1940 and the FBI had nothing to do with his service in the armed forces. He also testified that sometimes the FBI paid him about $1,000 a month for expenses. From the period 1942 to 1952, according to the Bureau records, Mazzei was paid the total of $172.05 as expense money.

Mazzei likewise testified that he had never been arrested in his life. In fact, he was arrested in connection with the paternity case brought against him in Pennsylvania by one Irene Corva. He has been arrested several times subsequent to this for his failure to make support payments to this woman.

On the argument of the motion the Solicitor General, in response to questions by the Court, stated with commendable candor that he believed the testimony given by Mazzei on June 18, 1953, before the Senate Committee concerning "the liquidation of Senator Joseph McCarthy" was untrue. He likewise stated that he believed the testimony given by Mazzei on July 2, 1956, in the Circuit Court of Florida was untrue. And in addition to the Solicitor General's personal opinion, the text of the motion itself shows that the Department of Justice is certain that some of Mazzei's post-trial testimony was contrary to the facts. The Pennsylvania statement of October 2, 1953, concerning his conviction of adultery and bastardy was controverted under oath at that hearing by an agent of the FBI. Mazzei again asserted in the Florida proceeding that he was induced to plead guilty to the adultery charge by an agent of the FBI. In the Florida testimony, he said that the FBI sometimes paid him a thousand dollars a month for expenses, whereas the records of the Bureau showed he was paid a total of $172.05 as expense money. He also testified there that the FBI arranged to put him in the Army to spy on a party member, whereas the FBI had nothing to do with his Army service; he had been inducted in accordance with the Selective Service Act. All these discrepancies are pointed out in the motion, as quoted above.

As to his bizarre testimony in the Florida proceeding concerning sabotage, espionage, handling of arms and ammunition, and plots to assassinate Senators, Congressmen and a state judge, the Government's motion suggests that none of it is worthy of belief by stating therein: "None of this testimony at the Florida proceeding is supported or corroborated by information in the possession of the Government."

At the oral argument, however, the Solicitor General stated that although he believed all of this testimony to be untrue, he was not prepared to say the witness Mazzei was guilty of perjury in giving the testimony; that his untrue statements might have been caused by a psychiatric condition, and that such condition might have arisen subsequent to the time of this trial. The Solicitor General, in the light of this position, asked to have the argument on the main case stricken from the calendar and the case remanded to the District Court for a full consideration of the credibility of the testimony of witness Mazzei. Commendable as the action of the Solicitor General was in promptly bringing the matter to our attention when it came to the attention of his office, we do not believe the disposition of the case suggested by him should be made.

Either this Court or the District Court should accept the statements of the Solicitor General as indicating the unreliability of this Government witness. The question of whether his untruthfulness in these other proceedings constituted perjury or was caused by a psychiatric condition can make no material difference here. Whichever explanation might be found to be correct in this regard, Mazzei's credibility has been wholly discredited by the disclosures of the Solicitor General. No other conclusion is possible. The dignity of the United States Government will not permit the conviction of any person on tainted testimony. This conviction is tainted, and there can be no other just result than to accord petitioners a new trial.

It must be remembered that we are not dealing here with a motion for a new trial initiated by the defense, under Rule 33 of the Federal Rules of Criminal Procedure, presenting untruthful statements by a Government witness subsequent to the trial as newly discovered evidence affecting his credibility at the trial. Such an allegation by the defense ordinarily will not support a motion for a new trial, because new evidence which is "merely cumulative or impeaching" is not, according to the often-repeated statement of the courts, an adequate basis for the grant of a new trial.

Here we have an entirely different situation. The witness

Mazzei was a paid informer of the Government—he had been in its employ from 1942 to 1953 for the purpose of infiltrating the Communist Party and reporting the facts found. He testified in this case in that capacity, as a Government witness. It is the Government which now questions the credibility of its own witness because in other proceedings in the same field of activity he gave certain testimony—some parts of it positively established as untrue and other parts of it believed by the Solicitor General to be untrue. The Solicitor General conceded that without Mazzei's testimony in this case the conviction of two of the petitioners cannot stand, but he argued that as to the other three Mazzei's evidence may not have had a substantial effect. But the trial judge believed Mazzei's testimony was material against them for, over objection, he admitted it against all the defendants. There were only seven witnesses. The testimony of Mazzei, at least, gave flesh-and-blood reality to the mass of Communist literature read to the jury to show advocacy of violence by the Communist Party. This being so, it cannot be determined conclusively by any court that his testimony was insignificant in the general case against the defendants. Thus it has tainted the trial as to all petitioners. As we said last Term in *Communist Party v. Subversive Activities Control Board:*

When uncontested challenge is made that a finding of subversive design by petitioner was in part the product of three perjurious witnesses, it does not remove the taint for a reviewing court to find that there is ample innocent testimony to support the Board's findings. If these witnesses in fact committed perjury in testifying in other cases on subject matter substantially like that of their testimony in the present proceedings, their testimony in this proceeding is inevitably discredited and the Board's determination must duly take this fact into account. [351 US 115, 124, 100 L ed 1003, 1009, 76 S Ct 663.]

There we remanded to the Subversive Activities Control Board for reconsideration of its original determination in the light of the record shorn of the tainted testimony. But there the Board, an administrative agency, was the original finder of fact. Here, on the other hand, in a criminal case, the original finder of fact was a jury. The district judge is not the proper agency to determine that there was sufficient evidence at the trial, other than that given by Mazzei, to sustain a conviction of any of the petitioners. Only the jury can determine what it would do on a different body of evidence, and the jury can no longer act in this case. For this reason, as well as that stated in the preceding paragraph, if on a remand the District Court should rule that the verdict against some of the petitioners could stand, we would be obliged, on a subsequent appeal, to reverse and, at that late date, direct that a new trial be granted. This case was instituted four and one half years ago; petitioners have been proceeding *in forma pauperis*. The interests of justice could not be served by a remand that must prove futile.

It might be different if we could see in this case any factual issue upon which the District Court, on a remand, could make an unassailable finding that Mazzei's other falsehoods were differentiated from his testimony herein. But it is not within the realm of reason to expect the district judge to determine, as the Government indicated it would ask him to do, that the witness Mazzei testified truthfully in this case in 1953 as an undercover informer concerning the activities of the Communist conspiracy, yet concurrently appeared in the same role in another tribunal and testified falsely—possibly because of a psychiatric condition—about a plan by different members of the Communist conspiracy to assassinate a United States Senator. That would be an unreasonable determination to make even though the judge might believe that Mazzei's bizarre testimony in 1956 concerning plans for the assassination of other officials, the destruction of bridges, training in sabotage and handling arms, and the poisoning of water in reservoirs, all to destroy the Government of the United States, was the product of a mental or emotional condition that had developed only after the time of this trial.

Mazzei, by his testimony, has poisoned the water in this reservoir, and the reservoir cannot be cleansed without first draining it of all impurity. This is a Federal criminal case, and this Court has supervisory jurisdiction over the proceedings of the Federal courts. If it has any duty to perform in this regard, it is to see that the waters of justice are not polluted. Pollution having taken place here, the condition should be remedied at the earliest opportunity.

The untainted administration of justice is certainly one of the most cherished aspects of our institutions. Its observance is one of our proudest boasts. This Court is charged with supervisory functions in relation to proceedings in the Federal courts. See McNabb v. United States, 318 US 332. Therefore, fastidious regard for the honor of the administration of justice requires the Court to make certain that the doing of justice be made so manifest that only irrational or perverse claims of its disregard can be asserted. [Communist Party v. Subversive Activities Control Board, 351 US 115, 124, 100 L ed 1003, 1009, 76 S Ct 663.]

The government of a strong and free nation does not need convictions based upon such testimony. It cannot afford to abide with them. The interests of justice call for a reversal of the judgments below with direction to grant the petitioners a new trial.

It is so ordered.

John T. Watkins v. United States of America
354 US 178, 1 L ed 2d 1273, 77 S Ct 1173

Decided June 17, 1957

John T. Watkins, a labor union official, appeared as a witness before a Subcommittee of the House Committee on Un-American Activities and refused to answer questions regarding past Communist Party membership of other persons. The refusal to answer was based on the ground that such questions were not pertinent to the Subcommittee's inquiry. Subsequently, he was convicted under a Federal statute providing for criminal punishment of witnesses before Congressional committees who refuse to answer pertinent questions. His conviction in the United States District Court for the District of Columbia was reversed, and then later affirmed, by the United States Court of Appeals for the District of Columbia Circuit.

Chief Justice Warren was joined by Justices Black, Douglas, Harlan and Brennan in holding that the conviction should be reversed because the evidence did not show that the subject under investigative inquiry at the time of *the questioning was made known to the witness. Justice Clark dissented. Justices Burton and Whittaker did not participate in the case.*

THIS IS A REVIEW by certiorari of a conviction under 2 USC § 192 for "contempt of Congress." The misdemeanor is alleged to have been committed during a hearing before a Congressional investigating committee. It is not the case of a truculent or contumacious witness who refuses to answer all questions or who, by boisterous or discourteous conduct, disturbs the decorum of the committee room. Petitioner was prosecuted for refusing to make certain disclosures which he asserted to be beyond the authority of the committee to demand. The controversy thus rests upon fundamental principles of the power of the Congress and the limitations upon that power. We approach the questions presented with conscious awareness of the far-reaching ramifications that can follow from a decision of this nature.

On April 29, 1954, petitioner appeared as a witness in compliance with a subpoena issued by a Subcommittee of the Committee on Un-American Activities of the House of Representatives. The Subcommittee elicited from petitioner a description of his background in labor union activities. He had been an employee of the International Harvester Company between 1935 and 1953. During the last eleven of those years, he had been on leave of absence to serve as an official of the Farm Equipment Workers International Union, later merged into the United Electrical, Radio and Machine Workers. He rose to the position of President of District No. 2 of the Farm Equipment Workers, a district defined geographically to include generally Canton and Rock

Falls, Illinois, and Dubuque, Iowa. In 1953, petitioner joined the United Auto Workers International Union as a labor organizer.

Petitioner's name had been mentioned by two witnesses who testified before the Committee at prior hearings. In September 1952, one Donald O. Spencer admitted having been a Communist from 1943 to 1946. He declared that he had been recruited into the party with the endorsement and prior approval of petitioner, whom he identified as the then District Vice-President of the Farm Equipment Workers. Spencer also mentioned that petitioner had attended meetings at which only card-carrying Communists were admitted. A month before petitioner testified, one Walter Rumsey stated that he had been recruited into the party by petitioner. Rumsey added that he had paid party dues to and later collected dues from petitioner, who had assumed the name Sam Brown. Rumsey told the Committee that he left the party in 1944.

Petitioner answered these allegations freely and without reservation. His attitude toward the inquiry is clearly revealed from the statement he made when the questioning turned to the subject of his past conduct, associations and predilections:

I am not now nor have I ever been a card-carrying member of the Communist Party. Rumsey was wrong when he said I had recruited him into the party, that I had received his dues, that I paid dues to him, and that I had used the alias Sam Brown.

Spencer was wrong when he termed any meetings which I attended as closed Communist Party meetings.

I would like to make it clear that for a period of time from approximately 1942 to 1947 I co-operated with the Communist Party and participated in Communist activities to such a degree that some persons may honestly believe that I was a member of the party.

I have made contributions upon occasions to Communist causes. I have signed petitions for Communist causes. I attended caucuses at an FE convention at which Communist Party officials were present.

Since I freely co-operated with the Communist Party I have no motive for making the distinction between co-operation and membership except the simple fact that it is the truth. I never carried a Communist Party card. I never accepted discipline and indeed on several occasions I opposed their position.

In a special convention held in the summer of 1947 I led the fight for compliance with the Taft-Hartley Act by the FE-CIO International Union. This fight became so bitter that it ended any possibility of future co-operation.

The character of petitioner's testimony on these matters can perhaps best be summarized by the Government's own appraisal in its brief:

A more complete and candid statement of his past political associations and activities (treating the Communist Party for present purposes as a mere political party) can hardly be imagined. Petitioner certainly was not attempting to conceal or withhold from the Committee his own past political associations, predilections, and preferences. Furthermore, petitioner told the Committee that he was entirely willing to identify for the Committee, and answer any questions it might have concerning "those persons whom I knew to be members of the Communist Party," provided that, "to [his] best knowledge and belief," they still were members of the Party. . . .

The Subcommittee, too, was apparently satisfied with petitioner's disclosures. After some further discussion elaborating on the statement, counsel for the Committee turned to another aspect of Rumsey's testimony. Rumsey had identified a group of persons whom he had known as members of the Communist Party, and counsel began to read this list of names to petitioner. Petitioner stated that he did not know several of the persons. Of those whom he did know, he refused to tell whether he knew them to have been members of the Communist Party. He explained to the Subcommittee why he took such a position:

I am not going to plead the Fifth Amendment, but I refuse to answer certain questions that I believe are outside the proper scope of your committee's activities. I will answer any questions which this committee puts to me about myself. I will also answer questions about those persons whom I knew to be members of the Communist Party and whom I believe still are. I will not, however, answer any questions with respect to others with whom I associated in the past. I do not believe that any law in this country requires me to testify about persons who may in the past have been Communist Party members or otherwise engaged in Communist Party activity but who to my best knowledge and belief have long since removed themselves from the Communist movement.

I do not believe that such questions are relevant to the work of this committee nor do I believe that this committee has the right to undertake the public exposure of persons because of their past activities. I may be wrong, and the committee may have this power, but until and unless a court of law so holds and directs me to answer, I most firmly refuse to discuss the political activities of my past associates.

The Chairman of the Committee submitted a report of petitioner's refusal to answer questions to the House of

Representatives. HR Rep No. 1579, 83d Cong, 2d Sess. The House directed the Speaker to certify the Committee's report to the United States Attorney for initiation of criminal prosecution. H Res 534, 83d Cong, 2d Sess. A seven-count indictment was returned. Petitioner waived his right to jury trial and was found guilty on all counts by the court. The sentence, a fine of $100 and one year in prison, was suspended, and petitioner was placed on probation.

An appeal was taken to the Court of Appeals for the District of Columbia. The conviction was reversed by a three-judge panel, one member dissenting. Upon rehearing en banc, the full bench affirmed the conviction, with the judges of the original majority in dissent. We granted certiorari because of the very important questions of constitutional law presented. 352 US 822, 1 L ed 2d 46, 77 S Ct 62.

We start with several basic premises on which there is general agreement. The power of the Congress to conduct investigations is inherent in the legislative process. That power is broad. It encompasses inquiries concerning the administration of existing laws as well as proposed or possibly needed statutes. It includes surveys of defects in our social, economic or political system for the purpose of enabling the Congress to remedy them. It comprehends probes into departments of the Federal Government to expose corruption, inefficiency or waste. But broad as is this power of inquiry, it is not unlimited. There is no general authority to expose the private affairs of individuals without justification in terms of the functions of the Congress. This was freely conceded by the Solicitor General in his argument of this case. Nor is the Congress a law enforcement or trial agency. These are functions of the executive and judicial departments of government. No inquiry is an end in itself; it must be related to and in furtherance of a legitimate task of the Congress. Investigations conducted solely for the personal aggrandizement of the investigators or to "punish" those investigated are indefensible.

It is unquestionably the duty of all citizens to co-operate with the Congress in its efforts to obtain the facts needed for intelligent legislative action. It is their unremitting obligation to respond to subpoenas, to respect the dignity of the Congress and its committees and to testify fully with respect to matters within the province of proper investigation. This, of course, assumes that the constitutional rights of witnesses will be respected by the Congress as they are in a court of justice. The Bill of Rights is applicable to investigations as to all forms of governmental action. Witnesses cannot be compelled to give evidence against themselves. They cannot be subjected to unreasonable search and seizure. Nor can the First Amendment freedoms of speech, press, religion, or political belief and association be abridged.

The rudiments of the power to punish for "contempt of Congress" come to us from the pages of English history. The origin of privileges and contempts extends back into the period of the emergence of Parliament. The establishment of a legislative body which could challenge the absolute power of the monarch is a long and bitter story. In that struggle, Parliament made broad and varied use of the contempt power. Almost from the beginning, both the House of Commons and the House of Lords claimed absolute and plenary authority over their privileges. This was an independent body of law, described by Coke as *lex parliamenti*. Only Parliament could declare what those privileges were or what new privileges were occasioned, and only Parliament could judge what conduct constituted a breach of privilege.

In particular, this exclusion of *lex parliamenti* from the *lex terrae*, or law of the land, precluded judicial review of the exercise of the contempt power or the assertion of privilege. Parliament declared that no court had jurisdiction to consider such questions. In the latter part of the seventeenth century, an action for false imprisonment was brought by one Jay who had been held in contempt. The defendant, the Serjeant at Arms of the House of Commons, demurred that he had taken the plaintiff into custody for breach of privilege. The Chief Justice, Pemberton, overruled the demurrer. Summoned to the bar of the House, the Chief Justice explained that he believed that the assertion of privilege went to the merits of the action and did not preclude jurisdiction. For his audacity, the Chief Justice was dispatched to Newgate prison.

It seems inevitable that the power claimed by Parliament would have been abused. Unquestionably it was. A few examples illustrate the way in which individual rights were infringed. During the seventeenth century, there was a violent upheaval, both religious and political. This was the time of the Reformation and the establishment of the Church of England. It was also the period when the Stuarts proclaimed that the royal prerogative was absolute. Ultimately there were two revolutions, one protracted and bloody, the second without bloodshed. Critical commentary of all kinds was treated as contempt of Parliament in these troubled days. Even clergymen were imprisoned for remarks made in their sermons. Perhaps the outstanding case arose from the private conversation of one Floyd, a Catholic, in which he expressed pleasure over the misfortune of the King's Protestant son-in-law and his wife. Floyd was not a member of Parliament. None of the persons concerned was in any way connected with the House of Commons. Nevertheless, that body imposed an humiliating and cruel sentence upon Floyd for contempt. The House of Lords intervened, rebuking the Commons for their extension of the privilege. The Commons acceded and transferred the record of the case to the Lords, who imposed substantially the same penalty.

Later in that century, during the reign of Charles II, there was great unrest over the fact that the heir apparent, James, had embraced Catholicism. Anti-Catholic feeling ran high, spilling over a few years later when the infamous rogue Titus Oates inflamed the country with rumors of a "Popish Plot" to murder the King. A committee of Parliament was appointed to learn the sources of certain pamphlets that had been appearing. One was entitled "The Grand Question Concerning the Prorogation of this Parliament for a Year and Three Months Stated and Discussed." A Doctor Carey admitted to the committee that he knew the author, but refused to divulge his name. Brought to the bar of the House of Lords, he persisted in this stand. The House imposed a fine of £1,000 and committed the witness to the Tower.

A hundred years later, George III had managed to gain control of Parliament through his ministers. The King could not silence the opposition, however, and one of the most vocal was John Wilkes. This precipitated a struggle that lasted for several years, until Wilkes finally prevailed. One writer sums up the case thus:

He had won a victory for freedom of the press. He had directed popular attention to the royally-controlled House of Commons, and pointed out its unrepresentative character, and had shown how easily a claim of privilege might be used to sanction the arbitrary proceedings of ministers and Parliament, even when a fundamental right of the subject was concerned. It is one of life's little ironies that work of such magnitude had been reserved for one of the worst libertines and demagogues of all time.

Even as late as 1835, the House of Commons appointed a select committee to inquire into ". . . the origin, nature, extent and tendency of the Orange Institutions." This was a political-religious organization, vehemently Protestant in religion and strongly in favor of the growth of the British Empire. The committee summoned the Deputy Grand Secretary and demanded that he produce all the records of the organization. The witness refused to turn over a letter book, which he admitted contained his answers to many communications upon Orange business. But it also contained, he said, records of private communications with respect to Orangcism. Summoned to the bar of the House of Commons, he remained adamant and was committed to Newgate prison.

Modern times have seen a remarkable restraint in the use by Parliament of its contempt power. Important investigations, like those conducted in America by Congressional committees, are made by Royal Commissions of Inquiry. These commissions are comprised of experts in the problem to be studied. They are removed from the turbulent forces of politics and partisan considerations. Seldom, if ever, have these commissions been given the authority to compel the testimony of witnesses or the production of documents. Their success in fulfilling their fact-finding missions without resort to coercive tactics is a tribute to the fairness of the processes to the witnesses and their close adherence to the subject matter committed to them.

The history of contempt of the legislature in this country is notably different from that of England. In the early days of the United States, there lingered the direct knowledge of the evil effects of absolute power. Most of the instances of use of compulsory process by the first Congresses concerned matters affecting the qualification or integrity of their members or came about in inquiries dealing with suspected corruption or mismanagement of government officials. Unlike the English practice, from the very outset the use of contempt power by the legislature was deemed subject to judicial review.

There was very little use of the power of compulsory process in early years to enable the Congress to obtain facts pertinent to the enactment of new statutes or the administration of existing laws. The first occasion for such an investigation arose in 1827 when the House of Representatives was considering a revision of the tariff laws. In the Senate, there was no use of a fact-finding investigation in aid of legislation until 1859. In the Legislative Reorganization Act, the Committee on Un-American Activities is the only standing committee of the House of Representatives that was given the power to compel disclosures.

It is not surprising, from the fact that the Houses of Congress so sparingly employed the power to conduct investigations, that there have been few cases requiring judicial review of the power. The nation was almost one hundred years old before the first case reached this Court to challenge the use of compulsory process as a legislative device, rather than in inquiries concerning the elections or privileges of Congressmen. In Kilbourn v. Thompson, 103 US 168, 26 L ed 377, decided in 1881, an investigation had been authorized by the House of Representatives to learn the circumstances surrounding the bankruptcy of Jay Cooke & Company, in which the United States had deposited funds. The committee became particularly interested in a private real-estate pool that was a part of the financial structure. The Court found that the subject matter of the inquiry was "in its nature clearly judicial and therefore one in respect to which no valid legislation could be enacted." The House had thereby exceeded the limits of its own authority.

Subsequent to the decision in *Kilbourn*, until recent times, there were very few cases dealing with the investigative power. The matter came to the fore again when the Senate undertook to study the corruption in handling of oil leases in the 1920s. In McGrain v. Daugherty, 273 US 135, 71 L ed 580, 47 S Ct 319, 50 ALR 1, and Sinclair v. United States, 279 US 263, 73 L ed 692, 49 S Ct 268, the Court applied the precepts of *Kilbourn* to uphold the authority of the Congress to conduct the challenged investigations. The Court recognized the danger to effective and honest conduct of the government if the legislature's power to probe corruption in the executive branch were unduly hampered.

Following these important decisions, there was another lull in judicial review of investigations. The absence of challenge, however, was not indicative of the absence of inquiries. To the contrary, there was vigorous use of the investigative process by a Congress bent upon harnessing and directing the vast economic and social forces of the times. Only one case came before this Court, and the authority of the Congress was affirmed.

In the decade following World War II, there appeared a new kind of Congressional inquiry unknown in prior periods of American history. Principally this was the result of the various investigations into the threat of subversion of the United States Government, but other subjects of Congressional interest also contributed to the changed scene. This new phase of legislative inquiry involved a broad-scale intrusion into the lives and affairs of private citizens. It brought before the courts novel questions of the appropriate limits of Congressional inquiry. Prior cases, like *Kilbourn*, *McGrain* and *Sinclair*, had defined the scope of investigative power in terms of the inherent limitations of the sources of that power. In the more recent cases, the emphasis shifted to problems of accommodating the interest of the government with the rights and privileges of individuals. The central theme was the application of the Bill of Rights as a restraint upon the assertion of governmental power in this form.

It was during this period that the Fifth Amendment privilege against self-incrimination was frequently invoked and recognized as a legal limit upon the authority of a committee to require that a witness answer its questions. Some early doubts as to the applicability of that privilege before a legislative committee never matured. When the matter reached this Court, the Government did not challenge in any way that the Fifth Amendment protection was available to the witness, and such a challenge could not have prevailed. It confined its argument to the character of the answers sought and to the adequacy of the claim of privilege. Quinn v. United States, 349 US 155, 99 L ed 964, 75 S Ct 668, 51 ALR2d 1157; Emspak v. United States, 349 US 190, 99 L ed 997, 75 S Ct 687; Bart v. United States, 349 US 219, 99 L ed 1016, 75 S Ct 712.

A far more difficult task evolved from the claim by witnesses that the committees' interrogations were infringements upon the freedoms of the First Amendment. Clearly, an investigation is subject to the command that the Congress shall make no law abridging freedom of speech or press or assembly. While it is true that there is no statute to be reviewed, and that an investigation is not a law, nevertheless an investigation is part of lawmaking. It is justified solely as an adjunct to the legislative process. The First Amendment may be invoked against infringement of the protected freedoms by law or by lawmaking.

Abuses of the investigative process may imperceptibly lead to abridgment of protected freedoms. The mere summoning of a witness and compelling him to testify, against his will, about his beliefs, expressions or associations is a measure of governmental interference. And when those forced revelations concern matters that are unorthodox, unpopular, or even hateful to the general public, the reaction in the life of the witness may be disastrous. This effect is even more harsh when it is past beliefs, expressions or associations that are disclosed and judged by current standards rather than those contemporary with the matters exposed. Nor does the witness alone suffer the consequences. Those who are identified by witnesses and thereby placed in the same glare of publicity are equally subject to public stigma, scorn and obloquy. Beyond that, there is the more subtle and immeasurable effect upon those who tend to adhere to the most orthodox and uncontroversial views and associations in order to avoid a similar fate at some future time. That this impact is partly the result of nongovernmental activity by private persons cannot relieve the investigators of their responsibility for initiating the reaction.

The Court recognized the restraints of the Bill of Rights upon Congressional investigations in United States v. Rumely, 345 US 41, 97 L ed 770, 73 S Ct 543. The magnitude and complexity of the problem of applying the First Amendment to that case led the Court to construe narrowly the resolution describing the Committee's authority. It was concluded that, when First Amendment rights are threatened, the delegation of power to the Committee must be clearly revealed in its charter.

Accommodation of the Congressional need for particular information with the individual and personal interest in privacy is an arduous and delicate task for any court. We do not underestimate the difficulties that would attend such an undertaking. It is manifest that despite the adverse effects which follow upon compelled disclosure of private matters, not all such inquiries are barred. *Kilbourn v. Thompson* teaches that such an investigation into individual affairs is invalid if unrelated to any legislative purpose. That is beyond the powers conferred upon the Congress in the Constitution. *United States v. Rumely* makes it plain that the mere semblance of legislative purpose would not justify an inquiry in the face of the Bill of Rights. The critical element is the existence of, and the weight to be ascribed to, the interest of the Congress in demanding disclosures from an unwilling witness. We cannot simply assume, however, that every Congressional investigation is justified by a public need that overbalances any private rights affected. To do so would be to abdicate the responsibility placed by the Constitution upon the judiciary to insure that the Congress does not unjustifiably encroach upon an individual's right to privacy nor abridge his liberty of speech, press, religion or assembly.

Petitioner has earnestly suggested that the difficult questions of protecting these rights from infringement by legislative inquiries can be surmounted in this case because there was no public purpose served in his interrogation. His conclusion is based upon the thesis that the Subcommittee was engaged in a program of exposure for the sake of exposure. The sole purpose of the inquiry, he contends, was to bring down upon himself and others the violence of public reaction because of their past beliefs, expressions and associations. In support of this argument, petitioner has marshaled an impressive array of evidence that some Congressmen have believed that such was their duty, or part of it.

We have no doubt that there is no Congressional power to expose for the sake of exposure. The public is, of course, entitled to be informed concerning the workings of its government. That cannot be inflated into a general power to expose where the predominant result can only be an invasion of the private rights of individuals. But a solution to our problem is not to be found in testing the motives of committee members for this purpose. Such is not our function. Their motives alone would not vitiate an investigation which has been instituted by a House of Congress if that assembly's legislative purpose is being served.

Petitioner's contentions do point to a situation of particular significance from the standpoint of the constitutional limitations upon Congressional investigations. The theory of a committee inquiry is that the committee members are serving as the representatives of the parent assembly in collecting information for a legislative purpose. Their function is to act as the eyes and ears of the Congress in obtaining facts upon which the full legislature can act. To carry out this mission, committees and subcommittees, sometimes one Congressman, are endowed with the full power of the Congress to compel testimony. In this case, only two men exercised that authority in demanding information over petitioner's protest.

An essential premise in this situation is that the House or Senate shall have instructed the committee members on what they are to do with the power delegated to them. It is the responsibility of the Congress, in the first instance, to insure that compulsory process is used only in furtherance of a legislative purpose. That requires that the instructions to an investigating committee spell out that group's jurisdiction and purpose with sufficient particularity. Those instructions are embodied in the authorizing resolution. That document is the committee's charter. Broadly drafted and loosely worded, however, such resolutions can leave tremendous latitude to the discretion of the investigators. The more vague the committee's charter is, the greater becomes the possibility that the committee's specific actions are not in conformity with the will of the parent House of Congress.

The authorizing resolution of the Un-American Activities Committee was adopted in 1938 when a select committee, under the chairmanship of Representative Dies, was created. Several years later, the Committee was made a standing organ of the House with the same mandate. It defines the Committee's authority as follows:

The Committee on Un-American Activities, as a whole or by subcommittee, is authorized to make from time to time investigations of (i) the extent, character, and objects of un-American propaganda activities in the United States, (ii) the diffusion within the United States of subversive and un-American propaganda that is instigated from foreign countries or of a domestic origin and attacks the principle of the form of government as guaranteed by our Constitution, and (iii) all other questions in relation thereto that would aid Congress in any necessary remedial legislation.

It would be difficult to imagine a less explicit authorizing resolution. Who can define the meaning of "un-American"? What is that single, solitary "principle of the form of government as guaranteed by our Constitution"? There is no need to dwell upon the language, however. At one time, perhaps, the resolution might have been read narrowly to confine the Committee to the subject of propaganda. The events that have transpired in the fifteen years before the interrogation of petitioner make such a construction impossible at this date.

The members of the Committee have clearly demonstrated that they did not feel themselves restricted in any way to propaganda in the narrow sense of the word. Unquestionably the Committee conceived of its task in the grand view of its name. Un-American activities were its target, no matter how or where manifested. Notwithstanding the broad purview of the Committee's experience, the House of Representatives repeatedly approved its continuation. Five times it extended the life of the special committee. Then it made the group a standing committee of the House. A year later, the Committee's charter was embodied in the Legislative Reorganization Act. On five occasions, at the beginning of sessions of Congress, it has made the authorizing resolution part of the rules of the House. On innumerable occasions, it has passed appropriation bills to allow the Committee to continue its efforts.

Combining the language of the resolution with the construction it has been given, it is evident that the preliminary control of the Committee exercised by the House of Representatives is slight or nonexistent. No one could reasonably deduce from the charter the kind of investigation that the Committee was directed to make. As a result, we are asked to engage in a process of retroactive rationalization. Looking backward from the events that transpired, we are asked to uphold the Committee's actions unless it appears that they were clearly not authorized by the charter. As a corollary to this inverse approach, the Government urges that we must view the matter hospitably to the power of the Congress— that if there is any legislative purpose which might have been furthered by the kind of disclosure sought, the witness must be punished for withholding it. No doubt every reasonable indulgence of legality must be accorded to the actions of a co-ordinate branch of our government. But such deference cannot yield to an unnecessary and unreasonable dissipation of precious constitutional freedoms.

The Government contends that the public interest at the core of the investigations of the Un-American Activities Committee is the need by the Congress to be informed of efforts to overthrow the government by force and violence so that adequate legislative safeguards can be erected. From this core, however, the Committee can radiate outward infinitely to any topic thought to be related in some way to armed insurrection. The outer reaches of this domain are known only by the content of "un-American activities." Remoteness of subject can be aggravated by a probe for a depth of detail even farther removed from any basis of legislative action. A third dimension is added when the investigators turn their attention to the past to collect minutiae on remote topics, on the hypothesis that the past may reflect upon the present.

The consequences that flow from this situation are manifold. In the first place, a reviewing court is unable to make the kind of judgment made by the Court in the United States v. Rumely (US) *supra*. The Committee is allowed, in essence, to define its own authority, to choose the direction and focus of its activities. In deciding what to do with the power that has been conferred upon them, members of the Committee may act pursuant to motives that seem to them to be the highest. Their decisions, nevertheless, can lead to ruthless exposure of private lives in order to gather data that is neither desired by the Congress nor useful to it. Yet it is impossible in this circumstance, with constitutional freedoms in jeopardy, to declare that the Committee has ranged beyond the area committed to it by its parent assembly, because the boundaries are so nebulous.

More important and more fundamental than that, however, it insulates the House that has authorized the investigation from the witnesses who are subjected to the sanctions of compulsory process. There is a wide gulf between the responsibility for the use of investigative power and the actual exercise of that power. This is an especially vital consideration in assuring respect for constitutional liberties. Protected freedoms should not be placed in danger in the absence of a clear determination by the House or the Senate that a particular inquiry is justified by a specific legislative need.

It is, of course, not the function of this Court to prescribe rigid rules for the Congress to follow in drafting resolutions establishing investigating committees. That is a matter peculiarly within the realm of the legislature, and its decisions will be accepted by the courts up to the point where their own duty to enforce the constitutionally protected rights of individuals is affected. An excessively broad charter, like that of the House Un-American Activities Committee, places the courts in an untenable position if they are to strike a balance between the public need for a particular interrogation and the right of citizens to carry on their affairs free from unnecessary governmental interference. It is impossible in such a situation to ascertain whether any legislative purpose justifies the disclosures sought and, if so, the importance of that information to the Congress in furtherance of its legislative function. The reason no court can make this critical judgment is that the House of Representatives itself has never made it. Only the legislative assembly initiating an investigation can assay the relative necessity of specific disclosures.

Absence of the qualitative consideration of petitioner's questioning by the House of Representatives aggravates a serious problem, revealed in this case, in the relationship of Congressional investigating committees and the witnesses who appear before them. Plainly these committees are restricted to the missions delegated to them i.e., to acquire certain data to be used by the House or the Senate in coping with a problem that falls within its legislative sphere. No witness can be compelled to make disclosures on matters outside that area. This is a jurisdictional concept of pertinency drawn from the nature of a Congressional committee's source of authority. It is not wholly different from nor unrelated to the element of pertinency embodied in the criminal statute under which petitioner was prosecuted. When the definition of jurisdictional pertinency is as uncertain and wavering as in the case the Un-American Activities Committee, it becomes extremely difficult for the Committee to limit its inquiries to statutory pertinency.

Since World War II, the Congress has practically abandoned its original practice of utilizing the coercive sanction of contempt proceedings at the bar of the House. The sanction there imposed is imprisonment by the House until the recalcitrant witness agrees to testify or disclose the matters sought, provided that the incarceration does not extend beyond adjournment. The Congress has instead invoked the aid of the Federal judicial system in protecting itself against contumacious conduct. It has become customary to refer these matters to the United States Attorneys for prosecution under criminal law.

The appropriate statute is found in 2 USC § 192. It provides:

Every person who having been summoned as a witness by the authority of either House of Congress to give testimony or to produce papers upon any matter under inquiry before either House, or any joint committee established by a joint or concurrent resolution of the two Houses of Congress, or any committee of either House of Congress, willfully makes default, or who, having appeared, refuses to answer any question pertinent to the question under inquiry, shall be deemed guilty of a misdemeanor, punishable by a fine of not more than $1,000 nor less than $100 and imprisonment in a common jail for not less than one month nor more than twelve months.

In fulfillment of their obligation under this statute, the courts must accord to the defendants every right which is guaranteed to defendants in all other criminal cases. Among these is the right to have available, through a sufficiently precise statute, information revealing the standard of criminality before the commission of the alleged offense. Applied to persons prosecuted under § 192, this raises a special problem in that the statute defines the crime as refusal to answer "any question pertinent to the question under inquiry." Part of the standard of criminality, therefore, is the pertinency of the questions propounded to the witness.

The problem attains proportion when viewed from the standpoint of the witness who appears before a Congressional committee. He must decide at the time the questions are propounded whether or not to answer. As the Court said in Sinclair v. United States, 279 US 263, 73 L ed 692, 49 S Ct 268, the witness acts at his peril. He is "bound rightly to construe the statute." *Idem*, 279 US at 299. An erroneous determination on his part, even if made in the utmost good faith, does not exculpate him if the court should later rule that the questions were pertinent to the question under inquiry.

It is obvious that a person compelled to make this choice is entitled to have knowledge of the subject to which the interrogation is deemed pertinent. That knowledge must be available with the same degree of explicitness and clarity that the Due Process Clause requires in the expression of any element of a criminal offense. The "vice of vagueness" must be avoided here as in all other crimes. There are several sources that can outline the "question under inquiry" in such a way that the rules against vagueness are satisfied. The authorizing resolution, the remarks of the chairman or members of the committee, or even the nature of the proceedings themselves might sometimes make the topic clear. This case demonstrates, however, that these sources often leave the matter in grave doubt.

The first possibility is that the authorizing resolution itself will so clearly declare the "question under inquiry" that a witness can understand the pertinency of questions asked him. The Government does not contend that the authorizing resolution of the Un-American Activities Committee could serve such a purpose. Its confusing breadth is amply illustrated by the innumerable and diverse questions into which the Committee has inquired under this charter since 1938. If the "question under inquiry" were stated with such sweeping and uncertain scope, we doubt that it would withstand an attack on the ground of vagueness.

That issue is not before us, however, in light of the Government's position that the immediate subject under inquiry before the Subcommittee interviewing petitioner was only one aspect of the Committee's authority to investigate un-American activities. Distilling that single topic from the broad field is an extremely difficult task upon the record before us. There was an opening statement by the Committee Chairman at the outset of the hearing, but this gives us no guidance. In this statement, the Chairman did no more than paraphrase the authorizing resolution and give a very general sketch of the past efforts of the Committee.

No aid is given as to the "question under inquiry" in the action of the full Committee that authorized the creation of the Subcommittee before which petitioner appeared. The Committee adopted a formal resolution giving the Chairman the power to appoint subcommittees ". . . for the purpose of performing any and all acts which the Committee as a whole is authorized to do." In effect, this was a device to enable the investigations to proceed with a quorum of one or two members and sheds no light on the relevancy of the questions asked of petitioner.

The Government believes that the topic of inquiry before the Subcommittee concerned Communist infiltration in labor. In his introductory remarks, the Chairman made reference to a bill, then pending before the Committee, which would have penalized labor unions controlled or dominated by persons who were, or had been, members of a "Communist-action" organization, as defined in the Internal Security Act of 1950. The Subcommittee, it is contended, might have been endeavoring to determine the extent of such a problem.

This view is corroborated somewhat by the witnesses who preceded and followed petitioner before the Subcommittee. Looking at the entire hearings, however, there is strong reason to doubt that the subject revolved about labor matters. The published transcript is entitled "Investigation of Communist Activities in the Chicago Area," and six of the nine witnesses had no connection with labor at all.

The most serious doubts as to the Subcommittee's "question under inquiry," however, stem from the precise questions that petitioner has been charged with refusing to answer. Under the terms of the statute, after all, it is these which must be proved pertinent. Petitioner is charged with refusing to tell the Subcommittee whether or not he knew that certain named persons had been members of the Communist Party in the past. The Subcommittee's counsel read the list from the testimony of a previous witness who had identified them as Communists. Although this former witness was identified with labor, he had not stated that the persons he named were involved in union affairs. Of the thirty names propounded to petitioner, seven were completely unconnected with organized labor. One operated a beauty parlor. Another was a watchmaker. Several were identified as "just citizens" or "only Communists." When almost a quarter of the persons on the list are not labor people, the inference becomes strong that the subject before the Subcommittee was not defined in terms of Communism in labor.

The final source of evidence as to the "question under inquiry" is the Chairman's response when petitioner objected to the questions on the grounds of lack of pertinency. The Chairman then announced that the Subcommittee was investigating "subversion and subversive propaganda." This is a subject at least as broad and indefinite as the authorizing resolution of the Committee, if not more so.

Having exhausted the several possible indicia of the "question under inquiry," we remain unenlightened as to the subject to which the questions asked petitioner were pertinent. Certainly, if the point is that obscure after trial and appeal, it was not adequately revealed to petitioner when he had to decide at his peril whether or not to answer. Fundamental fairness demands that no witness be compelled to make such a determination with so little guidance. Unless the subject matter has been made to appear with undisputable clarity, it is the duty of the investigative body, upon objection of the witness on grounds of pertinency, to state for the record the subject under inquiry at that time and the manner in which the propounded questions are pertinent thereto. To be meaningful, the explanation must describe what the topic under inquiry is and the connective reasoning whereby the precise questions asked relate to it.

The statement of the Committee Chairman in this case, in response to petitioner's protest, was woefully inadequate to convey sufficient information as to the pertinency of the questions to the subject under inquiry. Petitioner was thus not accorded a fair opportunity to determine whether he was within his rights in refusing to answer, and his conviction is necessarily invalid under the Due Process Clause of the Fifth Amendment.

We are mindful of the complexities of modern government and the ample scope that must be left to the Congress as the sole constitutional depository of legislative power. Equally mindful are we of the indispensable function, in the exercise of that power, of Congressional investigations. The conclusions we have reached in this case will not prevent the Congress, through its committees, from obtaining any information it needs for the proper fulfillment of its role in our scheme of government. The legislature is free to determine the kinds of data that should be collected. It is only those investigations that are conducted by use of compulsory process that give rise to a need to protect the rights of individuals against illegal encroachment. That protection can be readily achieved through procedures which prevent the separation of power from responsibility and which provide the constitutional requisites of fairness for witnesses. A measure of added care on the part of the House and the Senate in authorizing the use of compulsory process and by their committees in exercising that power would suffice. That is a small price to pay if it serves to uphold the principles of limited, constitutional government without constricting the power of the Congress to inform itself.

The judgment of the Court of Appeals is reversed, and the case is remanded to the District Court with instructions to dismiss the indictment.

It is so ordered.

Paul M. Sweezy v. State of New Hampshire
354 US 234, 1 L ed 2d 1311, 77 S Ct 1203

Decided June 17, 1957

At the invitation of members of the humanities faculty of the University of New Hampshire, Paul M. Sweezy had delivered lectures at the university. Subsequently, he was investigated and interrogated by the Attorney General of New Hampshire. When he refused to answer the questions of the Attorney General pertaining to his lectures and to the Progressive Party, the Attorney General had the questions put to him by the Superior Court of Merrimack County, New Hampshire. He continued his refusal to answer, was adjudged in contempt of court, and his conviction was upheld by the New Hampshire Supreme Court.

Chief Justice Warren was joined by Justices Black, Douglas and Brennan in holding that the conviction should be reversed because it violated due process of law as guaranteed by the Fourteenth Amendment. In a separate opinion, Justice Frankfurter, joined by Justice Harlan, concurred in the reversal of the conviction. Justice Clark, joined by Justice Burton, dissented. Justice Whittaker did not participate in the case.

THIS CASE, like Watkins v. United States, No. 261, also decided today [1 L ed 2d 1273] brings before us a question concerning the constitutional limits of legislative inquiry. The investigation here was conducted under the aegis of a state legislature, rather than a House of Congress. This places the controversy in a slightly different setting from that in Watkins. The ultimate question here is whether the investigation deprived Sweezy of due process of law under the Fourteenth Amendment. For the reasons to be set out in this opinion, we conclude that the record in this case does not sustain the power of the state to compel the disclosures that the witness refused to make.

This case was brought here as an appeal under 28 USC § 1257(2). Jurisdiction was alleged to rest upon contentions, rejected by the state courts, that a statute of New Hampshire is repugnant to the Constitution of the United States. We postponed a decision on the question of jurisdiction until consideration of the merits. 352 US 812, 77 S Ct 49. The parties neither briefed nor argued the jurisdictional question. The appellant has thus failed to meet his burden of showing that jurisdiction by appeal was properly invoked. The appeal is therefore dismissed. Treating the appeal papers as a petition for writ of certiorari, under 28 USC § 2103, the petition is granted. Cf. Union Nat. Bank v. Lamb, 337 US 38, 39, 40, 93 L ed 1190, 1193, 69 S Ct 911.

The investigation in which petitioner was summoned to testify had its origins in a statute passed by the New Hampshire Legislature in 1951. It was a comprehensive scheme of regulation of subversive activities. There was a section defining criminal conduct in the nature of sedition. "Subversive organizations" were declared unlawful and ordered dissolved. "Subversive persons" were made ineligible for employment by the state government. Included in the disability were those employed as teachers or in other capacities by any public educational institution. A loyalty program was instituted to eliminate "subversive persons" among government personnel. All present employees, as well as candidates for elective office in the future, were required to make sworn statements that they were not "subversive persons."

In 1953, the Legislature adopted a "Joint Resolution Relating to the Investigation of Subversive Activities." It was resolved:

That the Attorney General is hereby authorized and directed to make full and complete investigation with respect to violations of the subversive activities act of 1951 and to determine whether subversive persons as defined in said act are presently located within this state. The Attorney General is

*authorized to act upon his own motion and upon such infor-
mation as in his judgment may be reasonable or reliable. . . .*

*The Attorney General is directed to proceed with criminal
prosecutions under the subversive activities act whenever evidence presented to him in the course of the investigation indicates violation thereof, and he shall report to the 1955 session
on the first day of its regular session the results of his investigation, together with his recommendations, if any, for necessary legislation.*

Under state law, this was construed to constitute the
Attorney General as a one-man legislative committee. He
was given the authority to delegate any part of the investigation to any member of his staff. The Legislature conferred
upon the Attorney General the further authority to subpoena
witnesses or documents. He did not have power to hold witnesses in contempt, however. In the event that coercive or
punitive sanctions were needed, the Attorney General could
invoke the aid of a State Superior Court which could find
recalcitrant witnesses in contempt of court.

Petitioner was summoned to appear before the Attorney
General on two separate occasions. On January 5, 1954, peti-
tioner testified at length upon his past conduct and associa-
tions. He denied that he had ever been a member of the
Communist Party or that he had ever been part of any pro-
gram to overthrow the government by force or violence. The
interrogation ranged over many matters, from petitioner's
World War II military service with the Office of Strategic
Services to his sponsorship, in 1949, of the Scientific and
Cultural Conference for World Peace, at which he spoke.

During the course of the inquiry, petitioner declined to
answer several questions. His reasons for doing so were given
in a statement he read to the committee at the outset of
the hearing. He declared he would not answer those ques-

tions which were not pertinent to the subject under inquiry as well as those which transgress the limitations of the First Amendment. In keeping with this stand, he refused to disclose his knowledge of the Progressive Party in New Hampshire or of persons with whom he was acquainted in that organization. No action was taken by the Attorney General to compel answers to these questions.

The Attorney General again summoned petitioner to testify on June 3, 1954. There was more interrogation about the witness's prior contacts with Communists. The Attorney General lays great stress upon an article which petitioner had co-authored. It deplored the use of violence by the United States and other capitalist countries in attempting to preserve a social order which the writers thought must inevitably fall. This resistance, the article continued, will be met by violence from the oncoming socialism, violence which is to be less condemned morally than that of capitalism since its purpose is to create a "truly human society." Petitioner affirmed that he styled himself a "classical Marxist" and a "socialist" and that the article expressed his continuing opinion.

Again, at the second hearing, the Attorney General asked, and petitioner refused to answer, questions concerning the Progressive Party, and its predecessor, the Progressive Citizens of America. Those were:

Was she, Nancy Sweezy, your wife, active in the formation of the Progressive Citizens of America?

Was Nancy Sweezy then working with individuals who were then members of the Communist Party?

Was Charles Beebe active in forming the Progressive Citizens of America?

Was Charles Beebe active in the Progressive Party in New Hampshire?

Did he work with your present wife— Did Charles Beebe work with your present wife in 1947?

Did it [a meeting at the home of Abraham Walenko in Weare during 1948] have anything to do with the Progressive Party?

The Attorney General also turned to a subject which had not yet occurred at the time of the first hearing. On March 22, 1954, petitioner had delivered a lecture to a class of one hundred students in the humanities course at the University of New Hampshire. This talk was given at the invitation of the faculty teaching that course. Petitioner had addressed the class upon such invitations in the two preceding years as well. He declined to answer the following questions:

What was the subject of your lecture?

Didn't you tell the class at the University of New Hampshire on Monday, March 22, 1954, that socialism was inevitable in this country?

Did you advocate Marxism at that time?

Did you express the opinion, or did you make the statement at that time that socialism was inevitable in America?

Did you in this last lecture on March 22 or in any of the former lectures espouse the theory of dialectical materialism?

Distinct from the categories of questions about the Progressive Party and the lectures was one question about petitioner's opinions. He was asked: "Do you believe in Communism?" He had already testified that he had never been a member of the Communist Party, but he refused to answer this or any other question concerning opinion or belief.

Petitioner adhered in this second proceeding to the same reasons for not answering he had given in his statement at the first hearing. He maintained that the questions were not pertinent to the matter under inquiry and that they infringed upon an area protected under the First Amendment.

Following the hearings, the Attorney General petitioned the Superior Court of Merrimack County, New Hampshire, setting forth the circumstances of petitioner's appearance before the committee and his refusal to answer certain questions. The petition prayed that the court propound the questions to the witness. After hearing argument, the court ruled that the questions set out above were pertinent. Petitioner was called as a witness by the court and persisted in his refusal to answer for constitutional reasons. The court adjudged him in contempt and ordered him committed to the county jail until purged of the contempt.

The New Hampshire Supreme Court affirmed. 100 NH 103, 121 A2d 783. Its opinion discusses only two classes of questions addressed to the witness: those dealing with the lectures and those about the Progressive Party and the Progressive Citizens of America. No mention is made of the single question concerning petitioner's belief in communism. In view of what we hold to be the controlling issue of the case, however, it is unnecessary to resolve affirmatively that that particular question was or was not included in the decision by the State Supreme Court.

There is no doubt that legislative investigations, whether on a Federal or state level, are capable of encroaching upon the constitutional liberties of individuals. It is particularly important that the exercise of the power of compulsory process be carefully circumscribed when the investigative process tends to impinge upon such highly sensitive areas as freedom of speech or press, freedom of political association, and freedom of communication of ideas, particularly in the academic community. Responsibility for the proper conduct of investigations rests, of course, upon the legislature itself. If that assembly chooses to authorize inquiries on its behalf by a legislatively created committee, that basic responsibility carries forward to include the duty of adequate supervision of the actions of the committee. This safeguard can be nullified when a committee is invested with a broad and ill-defined jurisdiction. The authorizing resolution thus becomes especially significant in that it reveals the amount of discretion that has been conferred upon the committee.

In this case, the investigation is governed by provisions in the New Hampshire Subversive Activities Act of 1951. The Attorney General was instructed by the Legislature to look into violations of that act. In addition, he was given the far more sweeping mandate to find out if there were subversive persons, as defined in that act, present in New Hampshire. That statute, therefore, measures the breadth and scope of the investigation before us.

"Subversive persons" are defined in many gradations of conduct. Our interest is in the minimal requirements of that definition, since they will outline its reach. According to the statute, a person is a "subversive person" if he, by any means, aids in the commission of any act intended to assist in the alteration of the constitutional form of government by force or violence. The possible remoteness from armed insurrection of conduct that could satisfy these criteria is obvious from the language. The statute goes well beyond those who are engaged in efforts designed to alter the form of government by force or violence. The statute declares, in effect, that the assistant of an assistant is caught up in the definition. This chain of conduct attains increased significance in light of the lack of a necessary element of guilty knowledge in either stage of assistants. The State Supreme Court has held that the definition encompasses persons engaged in the specified conduct, "whether or not done

'knowingly and willfully. . . .' " Nelson v. Wyman, 99 NH
33, 39, 105 A2d 756. The potential sweep of this definition
extends to conduct which is only remotely related to actual
subversion and which is done completely free of any conscious intent to be a part of such activity.

The statute's definition of "subversive organizations" is
also broad. An association is said to be any group of persons,
whether temporarily or permanently associated together, for
joint action or advancement of views on any subject. An
organization is deemed subversive if it has a purpose to abet,
advise or teach activities intended to assist in the alteration
of the constitutional form of government by force or
violence.

The situation before us is in many respects analogous to
that in Wieman v. Updegraff, 344 US 183, 97 L ed 216, 73
S Ct 215. The Court held there that a loyalty oath prescribed
by the State of Oklahoma for all its officers and employees
violated the requirements of the Due Process Clause because
it entailed sanctions for membership in subversive organizations without *scienter*. A state cannot, in attempting to bar
disloyal individuals from its employ, exclude persons solely
on the basis of organizational membership, regardless of their
knowledge concerning the organizations to which they belonged. The Court said:

*There can be no dispute about the consequences visited
upon a person excluded from public employment on disloyalty grounds. In the view of the community, the stain is a
deep one; indeed, it has become a badge of infamy. Especially
is this so in time of cold war and hot emotions when "each
man begins to eye his neighbor as a possible enemy." Yet under the Oklahoma Act, the fact of association alone determines disloyalty and disqualification; it matters not whether*

*association existed innocently or knowingly. To thus inhibit
individual freedom of movement is to stifle the flow of democratic expression and controversy at one of its chief sources.*
[*344 US, at 190, 191.*]

The sanction emanating from legislative investigations is
of a different kind than loss of employment. But the stain of
the stamp of disloyalty is just as deep. The inhibiting effect
in the flow of democratic expression and controversy upon
those directly affected and those touched more subtly is
equally grave. Yet here, as in *Wieman*, the program for the
rooting out of subversion is drawn without regard to the
presence or absence of guilty knowledge in those affected.

The nature of the investigation which the Attorney General was authorized to conduct is revealed by this case. He
delved minutely into the past conduct of petitioner, thereby
making his private life a matter of public record. The
questioning indicates that the investigators had thoroughly
prepared for the interview and were not acquiring new information as much as corroborating data already in their
possession. On the great majority of questions, the witness
was co-operative, even though he made clear his opinion that
the interrogation was unjustified and unconstitutional. Two
subjects arose upon which petitioner refused to answer: his
lectures at the University of New Hampshire, and his knowledge of the Progressive Party and its adherents.

The state courts upheld the attempt to investigate the
academic subject on the ground that it might indicate
whether petitioner was a "subversive person." What he
taught the class at a state university was found relevant to
the character of the teacher. The State Supreme Court
carefully excluded the possibility that the inquiry was sustain-
able because of the state interest in the state university.

There was no warrant in the authorizing resolution for that. 100 NH, at 110, 121 A2d 783. The sole basis for the inquiry was to scrutinize the teacher as a person, and the inquiry must stand or fall on that basis.

The interrogation on the subject of the Progressive Party was deemed to come within the Attorney General's mandate because that party might have been shown to be a "subversive organization." The State Supreme Court held that the "questions called for answers concerning the membership or participation of named persons in the Progressive Party which, if given, would aid the Attorney General in determining whether that party and its predecessor are or were subversive organizations." 100 NH, at 112, 121 A2d 783.

The New Hampshire court concluded that:

[the] right to lecture and the right to associate with others for a common purpose, be it political or otherwise, are individual liberties guaranteed to every citizen by the State and Federal Constitutions but are not absolute rights. . . . The inquiries authorized by the Legislature in connection with this investigation concerning the contents of the lecture and the membership, purposes and activities of the Progressive Party undoubtedly interfered with the defendant's free exercise of those liberties. [100 NH, at 113, 121 A2d 783.]

The State Supreme Court thus conceded without extended discussion that petitioner's right to lecture and his right to associate with others were constitutionally protected freedoms which had been abridged through this investigation. These conclusions could not be seriously debated. Merely to summon a witness and compel him, against his will, to disclose the nature of his past expressions and associations is a measure of governmental interference in these matters. These are rights which are safeguarded by the Bill of Rights and the Fourteenth Amendment. We believe that there unquestionably was an invasion of petitioner's liberties in the areas of academic freedom and political expression—areas in which government should be extremely reticent to tread.

The essentiality of freedom in the community of American universities is almost self-evident. No one should underestimate the vital role in a democracy that is played by those who guide and train our youth. To impose any strait jacket upon the intellectual leaders in our colleges and universities would imperil the future of our nation. No field of education is so thoroughly comprehended by man that new discoveries cannot yet be made. Particularly is that true in the social sciences, where few, if any, principles are accepted as absolutes. Scholarship cannot flourish in an atmosphere of suspicion and distrust. Teachers and students must always remain free to inquire, to study and to evaluate, to gain new maturity and understanding; otherwise our civilization will stagnate and die.

Equally manifest as a fundamental principle of a democratic society is political freedom of the individual. Our form of government is built on the premise that every citizen shall have the right to engage in political expression and association. This right was enshrined in the First Amendment of the Bill of Rights. Exercise of these basic freedoms in America has traditionally been through the media of political associations. Any interference with the freedom of a party is simultaneously an interference with the freedom of its adherents. All political ideas cannot and should not be channeled into the programs of our two major parties. History has amply proved the virtue of political activity by minority, dissident groups, who innumerable times have been in the vanguard of democratic thought and whose programs were ultimately accepted. Mere unorthodoxy or dissent from the prevailing mores is not to be condemned. The absence of such voices would be a symptom of grave illness in our society.

Notwithstanding the undeniable importance of freedom in these areas, the Supreme Court of New Hampshire did not consider that the abridgment of petitioner's rights under the Constitution vitiated the investigation. In the view of that court, "the answer lies in a determination of whether the object of the legislative investigation under consideration is such as to justify the restriction thereby imposed upon the defendant's liberties." 100 NH, at 113, 114, 121 A2d 783. It found such justification in the Legislature's judgment, expressed by its authorizing resolution, that there exists a potential menace from those who would overthrow the government by force and violence. That court concluded that the need for the Legislature to be informed on so elemental a subject as the self-preservation of government outweighed the deprivation of constitutional rights that occurred in the process.

We do not now conceive of any circumstance wherein a state interest would justify infringement of rights in these fields. But we do not need to reach such fundamental questions of state power to decide this case. The State Supreme Court itself recognized that there was a weakness in its conclusion that the menace of forcible overthrow of the government justified sacrificing constitutional rights. There was a missing link in the chain of reasoning. The syllogism was not complete. There was nothing to connect the questioning of petitioner with this fundamental interest of the state. Petitioner had been interrogated by a one-man legislative committee, not by the Legislature itself. The relationship of the committee to the full assembly is vital, therefore, as revealing the relationship of the questioning to the state interest.

In light of this, the state court emphasized a factor in the authorizing resolution which confined the inquiries which the Attorney General might undertake to the object of the investigation. That limitation was thought to stem from the authorizing resolution's condition precedent to the institution of any inquiry. The New Hampshire Legislature specified that the Attorney General should act only when he had information which "in his judgment may be reasonable or reliable." The state court construed this to mean that the Attorney General must have something like probable cause for conducting a particular investigation. It is not likely that this device would prove an adequate safeguard against unwarranted inquiries. The Legislature has specified that the determination of the necessity for inquiry shall be left in the judgment of the investigator. In this case, the record does not reveal what reasonable or reliable information led the Attorney General to question petitioner. The state court relied upon the Attorney General's description of prior information that had come into his possession.

The respective roles of the Legislature and the investigator thus revealed are of considerable significance to the issue before us. It is eminently clear that the basic discretion of determining the direction of the legislative inquiry has been turned over to the investigative agency. The Attorney General has been given such a sweeping and uncertain mandate that it is his decision which picks out the subjects that will be pursued, what witnesses will be summoned and what questions will be asked. In this circumstance, it cannot be stated authoritatively that the Legislature asked the Attorney General to gather the kind of facts comprised in the subjects upon which petitioner was interrogated.

188

Instead of making known the nature of the data it desired, the Legislature has insulated itself from those witnesses whose rights may be vitally affected by the investigation. Incorporating by reference provisions from its Subversive Activities Act, it has told the Attorney General, in effect, to screen the citizenry of New Hampshire to bring to light anyone who fits into the expansive definitions.

Within the very broad area thus committed to the discretion of the Attorney General there may be many facts which the Legislature might find useful. There would also be a great deal of data which that assembly would not want or need. In the classes of information that the Legislature might deem it desirable to have, there will be some which it could not validly acquire because of the effect upon the constitutional rights of individual citizens. Separating the wheat from the chaff, from the standpoint of the Legislature's object, is the Legislature's responsibility because it alone can make that judgment. In this case, the New Hampshire Legislature has delegated that task to the Attorney General.

As a result neither we nor the state courts have any assurance that the questions petitioner refused to answer fall into a category of matters upon which the Legislature wanted to be informed when it initiated this inquiry. The judiciary are thus placed in an untenable position. Lacking even the elementary fact that the Legislature wants certain questions answered and recognizing that petitioner's constitutional rights are in jeopardy, we are asked to approve or disapprove his incarceration for contempt.

In our view, the answer is clear. No one would deny that the infringement of constitutional rights of individuals would violate the guarantee of due process where no state interest underlies the state action. Thus, if the Attorney General's interrogation of petitioner were in fact wholly unrelated to the object of the Legislature in authorizing the inquiry, the Due Process Clause would preclude the endangering of constitutional liberties. We believe that an equivalent situation is presented in this case. The lack of any indications that the Legislature wanted the information the Attorney General attempted to elicit from petitioner must be treated as the absence of authority. It follows that the use of the contempt power, notwithstanding the interference with constitutional rights, was not in accordance with the due-process requirements of the Fourteenth Amendment.

The conclusion that we have reached in this case is not grounded upon the doctrine of separation of powers. In the Federal Government, it is clear that the Constitution has conferred the powers of government upon three major branches: the executive, the legislative and the judicial. No contention has been made by petitioner that the New Hampshire Legislature, by this investigation, arrogated to itself executive or judicial powers. We accept the finding of the State Supreme Court that the employment of the Attorney General as the investigating committee does not alter the legislative nature of the proceedings. Moreover, this Court has held that the concept of separation of powers embodied in the United States Constitution is not mandatory in state governments. Dreyer v. Illinois, 187 US 71, 47 L ed 79, 23 S Ct 28; but cf. Tenney v. Brandhove, 341 US 367, 378, 95 L ed 1019, 1027, 71 S Ct 783. Our conclusion does rest upon a separation of the power of a state legislature to conduct investigations from the responsibility to direct the use of that power insofar as that separation causes a deprivation of the constitutional rights of individuals and a denial of due process of law.

The judgment of the Supreme Court of New Hampshire is Reversed.

Albert L. Trop v. John Foster Dulles,
Secretary of State of the United States
of America
356 US 86, 2 L ed 2d 630, 78 S Ct 590

Decided March 31, 1958

The application of Albert L. Trop for a passport was denied on the ground that, under the provisions of the Nationality Act of 1940, he had lost his citizenship because of his court-martial conviction and dishonorable discharge from the United States Army for wartime desertion. He then sought a declaratory judgment that he was a citizen, which was refused by the United States District Court for the Eastern District of New York. This decision was affirmed by the United States Court of Appeals for the Second Circuit.

Chief Justice Warren was joined by Justices Black, Douglas and Whittaker in holding that the national government does not have such powers to divest citizenship, and that, in addition, the Eighth Amendment does not permit the divesting of citizenship to be used as a punishment. In a separate opinion, Justice Brennan concurred as to the reversal of lower-court action. Justice Frankfurter, joined by Justices Burton, Clark and Harlan, dissented.

THE PETITIONER in this case, a native-born American, is declared to have lost his United States citizenship and becomes stateless by reason of his conviction by court-martial for wartime desertion. As in Perez v. Brownell, 2 L ed 2d 603, the issue before us is whether this forfeiture of citizenship comports with the Constitution.

The facts are not in dispute. In 1944 petitioner was a private in the United States Army, serving in French Morocco. On May 22, he escaped from a stockade at Casablanca, where he had been confined following a previous breach of discipline. The next day petitioner and a companion were walking along a road toward Rabat, in the general direction back to Casablanca, when an Army truck approached and stopped. A witness testified that petitioner boarded the truck willingly and that no words were spoken. In Rabat petitioner was turned over to military police. Thus ended petitioner's "desertion." He had been gone less than a day and had willingly surrendered to an officer of an Army vehicle while he was walking back toward his base. He testified that at the time he and his companion were picked up by the Army truck, "we had decided to return to the stockade. The going was tough. We had no money to speak of, and at the time we were on foot and we were getting cold and hungry." A general court-martial convicted petitioner of desertion and sentenced him to three years of hard labor, forfeiture of all pay and allowances and a dishonorable discharge.

In 1952 petitioner applied for a passport. His application was denied on the ground that under the provisions of Section 401 (g) of the Nationality Act of 1940, as amended, he had lost his citizenship by reason of his conviction and dishonorable discharge for wartime desertion. In 1955 petitioner commenced this action in the District Court, seeking a declaratory judgment that he is a citizen. The government's motion for summary judgment was granted, and the Court of Appeals for the Second Circuit affirmed, Chief Judge Clark dissenting. 239 F2d 527. We granted certiorari. 352 US 1023, 1 L ed 2d 596, 77 S Ct 591.

Section 401 (g), the statute that decrees the forfeiture of this petitioner's citizenship, is based directly on a Civil War statute, which provided that a deserter would lose his "rights of citizenship." The meaning of this phrase was not clear. When the 1940 codification and revision of the nationality laws was prepared, the Civil War statute was amended to make it certain that what a convicted deserter would lose was nationality itself. In 1944 the statute was further amended to provide that a convicted deserter would lose his citizenship only if he was dismissed from the service or dishonorably discharged. At the same time it was provided that citizenship could be regained if the deserter was restored to active duty in wartime with the permission of the military authorities.

Though these amendments were added to ameliorate the harshness of the statute, their combined effect produces a result that poses far graver problems than the ones that were sought to be solved. Section 401 (g) as amended now gives the military authorities complete discretion to decide who among convicted deserters shall continue to be Americans and who shall be stateless. By deciding whether to issue and execute a dishonorable discharge and whether to allow a deserter to re-enter the armed forces, the military becomes the arbiter of citizenship. And the domain given to it by Congress is not as narrow as might be supposed. Though the crime of desertion is one of the most serious in military law, it is by no means a rare event for a soldier to be convicted of this crime. The elements of desertion are simply absence from duty plus the intention not to return. Into this category falls a great range of conduct, which may be prompted by a variety of motives—fear, laziness, hysteria or any emotional imbalance. The offense may occur not only in combat but also in training camps for draftees in this country. The Solicitor General informed the Court that during World War II, according to Army estimates, approximately 21,000 soldiers and airmen were convicted of desertion and given dishonorable discharges by the sentencing courts-martial and that about 7,000 of these were actually separated from the service and thus rendered stateless when the reviewing authorities refused to remit their dishonorable discharges. Over this group of men, enlarged by whatever the corresponding figures may be for the Navy and Marines, the military has been given the power to grant or withhold citizenship. And the number of youths subject to this power could easily be enlarged simply by expanding the statute to cover crimes other than desertion. For instance, a dishonorable discharge itself might in the future be declared to be sufficient to justify forfeiture of citizenship.

Three times in the past three years we have been confronted with cases presenting important questions bearing on the proper relationship between civilian and military authority in this country. A statute such as Section 401 (g) raises serious issues in this area, but in our view of this case it is unnecessary to deal with those problems. We conclude that the judgment in this case must be reversed for the following reasons.

I

In Perez v. Brownell (US) supra, I expressed the principles that I believe govern the constitutional status of United States citizenship. It is my conviction that citizenship is not subject to the general powers of the national government and therefore cannot be divested in the exercise of those powers. The right may be voluntarily relinquished or abandoned either by express language or by language and conduct that show a renunciation of citizenship.

Under these principles, this petitioner has not lost his citizenship. Desertion in wartime, though it may merit the ultimate penalty, does not necessarily signify allegiance to a foreign state. Section 401 (g) is not limited to cases of desertion to the enemy, and there is no such element in this case. This soldier committed a crime for which he should be and was punished, but he did not involve himself in any way with a foreign state. There was no dilution of his allegiance to this country. The fact that the desertion occurred on foreign soil is of no consequence. The Solicitor General acknowledged that forfeiture of citizenship would have occurred if the entire incident had transpired in this country.

Citizenship is not a license that expires upon misbehavior. The duties of citizenship are numerous, and the discharge of many of these obligations is essential to the security and well-being of the nation. The citizen who fails to pay his taxes or to abide by the laws safeguarding the integrity of elections deals a dangerous blow to his country. But could a citizen be deprived of his nationality for evading these basic responsibilities of citizenship? In time of war the citizen's duties include not only the military defense of the nation but also full participation in the manifold activities of the civilian ranks. Failure to perform any of these obligations may cause the nation serious injury, and, in appropriate circumstances, the punishing power is available to deal with derelictions of duty. But citizenship is not lost every time a duty of citizenship is shirked. And the deprivation of citizenship is not a weapon that the government may use to express its displeasure at a citizen's conduct, however reprehensible that conduct may be. As long as a person does not voluntarily renounce or abandon his citizenship, and this petitioner has done neither, I believe his fundamental right of citizenship is secure. On this ground alone the judgment in this case should be reversed.

II

Since a majority of the Court concluded in *Perez v. Brownell* that citizenship may be divested in the exercise of some governmental power, I deem it appropriate to state additionally why the action taken in this case exceeds constitutional limits, even under the majority's decision in *Perez*. The Court concluded in *Perez* that citizenship could be divested in the exercise of the foreign-affairs power. In this case, it is urged that the war power is adequate to support the divestment of citizenship. But there is a vital difference between the two statutes that purport to implement these powers by decreeing loss of citizenship. The statute in *Perez* decreed loss of citizenship—so the majority concluded—to eliminate those international problems that were thought to arise by reason of a citizen's having voted in a foreign election. The statute in this case, however, is entirely different. Section 401 (g) decrees loss of citizenship for those found guilty of the crime of desertion. It is essentially like Section 401 (j) of the Nationality Act, decreeing loss of citizenship for evading the draft by remaining outside the United States. This provision was also before the Court in *Perez*, but the majority declined to consider its validity. While Section 401 (j) decrees loss of citizenship without providing any semblance of procedural due process whereby the guilt of the draft evader may be determined before the sanction is imposed, Section 401 (g), the provision in this case, accords the accused deserter at least the safeguards of an adjudication of guilt by a court-martial.

The constitutional question posed by Section 401 (g) would appear to be whether or not denationalization may be inflicted as a punishment, even assuming that citizenship may be divested pursuant to some governmental power. But the Government contends that this statute does not impose a penalty and that constitutional limitations on the power of Congress to punish are therefore inapplicable. We are told this is so because a committee of cabinet members, in recommending this legislation to the Congress, said it "technically is not a penal law." How simple would be the tasks of constitutional adjudication and of law generally if specific problems could be solved by inspection of the labels pasted on them! Manifestly the issue of whether Section 401 (g) is a penal law cannot be thus determined. Of course it is relevant to know the classification employed by the cabinet committee that played such an important role in the preparation of the Nationality Act of 1940. But it is equally relevant to know that this very committee acknowledged that Section 401 (g) was based on the provisions of the 1865 Civil War statute, which the committee itself termed "distinctly penal in character." Furthermore, the 1865 statute states in terms that deprivation of the rights of citizenship is "in addition to the other lawful penalties of the crime of desertion . . ." And certainly it is relevant to know that the reason given by the Senate Committee on Immigration as to why loss of nationality under Section 401 (g) can follow desertion only after conviction by court-martial was "because the penalty is so drastic." Doubtless even a clear legislative classification of a statute as "nonpenal" would not alter the fundamental nature of a plainly penal statute. With regard to Section 401 (g) the fact is that the views of the cabinet committee and of the Congress itself as to the nature of the statute are equivocal and cannot possibly provide the answer to our inquiry. Determination of whether this statute is a penal law requires careful consideration.

In form Section 401 (g) appears to be a regulation of nationality. The statute deals initially with the status of nationality and then specifies the conduct that will result in loss of that status. But surely form cannot provide the answer to this inquiry. A statute providing that "a person shall lose his liberty by committing bank robbery," though in form a regulation of liberty, would nonetheless be penal. Nor would its penal effect be altered by labeling it a regulation of banks or by arguing that there is a rational connection between safeguarding banks and imprisoning bank robbers. The inquiry must be directed to substance.

This Court has been called upon to decide whether or not various statutes were penal ever since 1798. Calder v. Bull (US) 3 Dall 386, 1 L ed 648. Each time a statute has been challenged as being in conflict with the constitutional prohibitions against bills of attainder and ex post facto laws, it has been necessary to determine whether a penal law was involved, because these provisions apply only to statutes imposing penalties. In deciding whether or not a law is penal, this Court has generally based its determination upon the purpose of the statute. If the statute imposes a disability for the purposes of punishment—that is, to reprimand the wrongdoer, to deter others, etc.—it has been considered penal. But a statute has been considered nonpenal if it imposes a disability, not to punish, but to accomplish some other legitimate governmental purpose. The Court has recognized that any statute decreeing some adversity as a consequence of certain conduct may have both a penal and a nonpenal effect. The controlling nature of such statutes normally depends on the evident purpose of the legislature. The point may be illustrated by the situation of an ordinary felon. A person who commits a bank robbery, for instance, loses his right to liberty and often his right to vote. If, in the exercise of the power to protect banks, both sanctions were imposed for the purpose of punishing bank robbers, the statutes authorizing both disabilities would be penal. But because the purpose of the latter statute is to designate a reasonable ground of eligibility for voting, this law is sustained as a nonpenal exercise of the power to regulate the franchise.

The same reasoning applies to Section 401 (g). The purpose of taking away citizenship from a convicted deserter is simply to punish him. There is no other legitimate purpose that the statute could serve. Denationalization in this case is not even claimed to be a means of solving international problems, as was argued in *Perez*. Here the purpose is punishment, and therefore the statute is a penal law.

It is urged that this statute is not a penal law but a regulatory provision authorized by the war power. It cannot be denied that Congress has power to prescribe rules governing the proper performance of military obligations, of which perhaps the most significant is the performance of one's duty when hazardous or important service is required. But a statute that prescribes the consequence that will befall one who fails to abide by these regulatory provisions is a penal law. Plainly legislation prescribing imprisonment for the crime of desertion is penal in nature. If loss of citizenship is substituted for imprisonment, it cannot fairly be said that the use of this particular sanction transforms the fundamental nature of the statute. In fact, a dishonorable discharge with consequent loss of citizenship might be the only punishment meted out by a court-martial. During World War II the threat of this punishment was explicitly communicated by the Army to soldiers in the field. If this statute taking away citizenship is a Congressional exercise of the war power, then it cannot rationally be treated other than as a penal law, because it imposes the sanction of denationalization for the purpose of punishing transgression of a standard of conduct prescribed in the exercise of that power.

The Government argues that the sanction of denationalization imposed by Section 401 (g) is not a penalty because deportation has not been so considered by this Court. While deportation is undoubtedly a harsh sanction that has a severe penal effect, this Court has in the past sustained deportation as an exercise of the sovereign's power to determine the conditions upon which an alien may reside in this country. For example, the statute authorizing deportation of an alien convicted under the 1917 Espionage Act was viewed not as designed to punish him for the crime of espionage, but as an implementation of the sovereign power to exclude, from which the deporting power is derived. Mahler v. Eby, 264 US 32, 68 L ed 549, 44 S Ct 283. This view of deportation may be highly fictional, but even if its validity is conceded, it is wholly inapplicable to this case. No one contends that the government has, in addition to the power to exclude all aliens, a sweeping power to denationalize all citizens. Nor does comparison to denaturalization eliminate the penal effect of denationalization in this case. Denaturalization is not imposed to penalize the alien for having falsified his application for citizenship; if it were, it would be a punishment. Rather, it is imposed in the exercise of the power to make rules for the naturalization of aliens. In short, the fact that deportation and denaturalization for fraudulent procurement of citizenship may be imposed for purposes other than punishment affords no basis for saying that in this case denationalization is not a punishment.

Section 401 (g) is a penal law, and we must face the question whether the Constitution permits the Congress to take away citizenship as a punishment for crime. If it is assumed that the power of Congress extends to divestment of citizenship, the problem still remains as to this statute whether denationalization is a cruel and unusual punishment within the meaning of the Eighth Amendment. Since wartime desertion is punishable by death, there can be no argument that the penalty of denationalization is excessive in relation to the gravity of the crime. The question is whether this penalty subjects the individual to a fate forbidden by the principle of civilized treatment guaranteed by the Eighth Amendment.

At the outset, let us put to one side the death penalty as an index of the constitutional limit on punishment. Whatever the arguments may be against capital punishment, both on moral grounds and in terms of accomplishing the purposes of punishment—and they are forceful—the death penalty has been employed throughout our history; and in a day when it is still widely accepted, it cannot be said to violate the constitutional concept of cruelty. But it is equally plain that the existence of the death penalty is not a license to the government to devise any punishment short of death within the limit of its imagination.

The exact scope of the constitutional phrase "cruel and unusual" has not been detailed by this Court. But the basic policy reflected in these words is firmly established in the Anglo-American tradition of criminal justice. The phrase in our Constitution was taken directly from the English Declaration of Rights of 1688, and the principle it represents can be traced back to the Magna Charta. The basic concept underlying the Eighth Amendment is nothing less than the dignity of man. While the state has the power to punish, the Amendment stands to assure that this power be exercised within the limits of civilized standards. Fines, imprisonment and even execution may be imposed depending upon the enormity of the crime, but any technique outside the bounds of these traditional penalties is constitutionally suspect. This Court has had little occasion to give precise content to the Eighth Amendment, and in an enlightened democracy such as ours this is not surprising. But when the Court was confronted with a punishment of twelve years in irons at hard and painful labor imposed for the crime of falsifying public records, it did not hesitate to declare that the penalty was cruel in its excessiveness and unusual in its character. Weems v. United States, 217 US 349, 54 L ed 793 30 S Ct 544, 19 Ann Cas 705. The Court recognized in that case that the words of the Amendment are not precise, and that their scope is not static. The Amendment must draw its meaning from the evolving standards of decency that mark the progress of a maturing society.

We believe, as did Chief Judge Clark in the court below, that use of denationalization as a punishment is barred by the Eighth Amendment. There may be involved no physical mistreatment, no primitive torture. There is instead the total destruction of the individual's status in organized society. It is a form of punishment more primitive than torture, for it destroys for the individual the political existence that was centuries in the development. The punishment strips the citizen of his status in the national and international political community. His very existence is at the sufferance of the country in which he happens to find himself. While any one country may accord him some rights—and presumably as long as he remained in this country he would enjoy the limited rights of an alien—no country need do so, because he is stateless. Furthermore, his enjoyment of even the limited rights of an alien might be subject to termination at any time by reason of deportation. In short, the expatriate has lost the right to have rights.

This punishment is offensive to cardinal principles for which the Constitution stands. It subjects the individual to a fate of ever increasing fear and distress. He knows not what discriminations may be established against him, what proscriptions may be directed against him, and when and for what cause his existence in his native land may be terminated. He may be subject to banishment, a fate universally decried by civilized people. He is stateless, a condition deplored in the international community of democracies. It is no answer to suggest that all the disastrous consequences of this fate may not be brought to bear on a stateless person. The threat makes the punishment obnoxious.

The civilized nations of the world are in virtual unanimity that statelessness is not to be imposed as punishment for crime. It is true that several countries prescribe expatriation in the event that their nationals engage in conduct in derogation of native allegiance. Even statutes of this sort are generally applicable primarily to naturalized citizens. But use of denationalization as punishment for crime is an entirely different matter. The United Nations' survey of the nationality laws of eighty-four nations of the world reveals that only two countries, the Philippines and Turkey, impose denationalization as a penalty for desertion. In this country the Eighth Amendment forbids this to be done.

In concluding as we do that the Eighth Amendment forbids Congress to punish by taking away citizenship, we are mindful of the gravity of the issue inevitably raised whenever the constitutionality of an act of the national legislature is challenged. No member of the Court believes that in this case the statute before us can be construed to avoid the issue of constitutionality. That issue confronts us, and the task of resolving it is inescapably ours. This task requires the exercise of judgment, not the reliance upon personal preferences. Courts must not consider the wisdom of statutes but neither can they sanction as being merely unwise that which the Constitution forbids.

We are oath-bound to defend the Constitution. This obligation requires that Congressional enactments be judged by the standards of the Constitution. The judiciary has the duty of implementing the constitutional safeguards that protect individual rights. When the government acts to take away the fundamental right of citizenship, the safeguards of the Constitution should be examined with special diligence.

The provisions of the Constitution are not timeworn adages or hollow shibboleths. They are vital, living principles that authorize and limit governmental powers in our nation. They are the rules of government. When the constitutionality of an act of Congress is challenged in this Court, we must apply those rules. If we do not, the words of the Constitution become little more than good advice.

When it appears that an act of Congress conflicts with one of these provisions, we have no choice but to enforce the paramount commands of the Constitution. We are sworn to do no less. We cannot push back the limits of the Constitution merely to accommodate challenged legislation. We must apply those limits as the Constitution prescribes them, bearing in mind both the broad scope of legislative discretion and the ultimate responsibility of constitutional adjudication. We do well to approach this task cautiously, as all our predecessors have counseled. But the ordeal of judgment cannot be shirked. In some eighty-one instances since this Court was established it has determined that Congressional action exceeded the bounds of the Constitution. It is so in this case.

The judgment of the Court of Appeals for the Second Circuit is reversed and the cause is remanded to the District Court for appropriate proceedings.

Reversed and remanded.

The Chief Justice Dissents

Cecil Reginald Jay v. John P. Boyd,
District Director, Immigration and
Naturalization Service

351 US 345, 100 L ed 1242, 76 S Ct 919

Decided June 11, 1956

Cecil Reginald Jay, an alien, was ordered deported from the
United States because of Communist Party membership
from 1935 to 1940. Although he met the requirements for
suspension of deportation as provided for in the Immigration
and Nationality Act of 1952, his application for suspension
of deportation was denied by the Immigration and Naturalization Service on the basis of undisclosed confidential information. His application for a writ of habeas corpus was
denied by the United States District Court for the Western
District of Washington, and the refusal of habeas corpus
was affirmed by the United States Court of Appeals for the
Ninth Circuit.

Justice Reed was joined by Justices Burton, Clark, Minton
and Harlan in holding that the denial of the application for

suspension of deportation was proper. In separate opinions, Chief Justice Warren and Justices Black, Frankfurter and Douglas each dissented.

In CONSCIENCE, I cannot agree with the opinion of the majority. It sacrifices to form too much of the American spirit of fair play in both our judicial and administrative processes.

In the interest of humanity, the Congress, in order to relieve some of the harshness of the immigration laws, gave the Attorney General discretion to relieve hardship in deportation cases. I do not believe it was "an unfettered discretion," as stated in the opinion. It was an administrative discretion calling for a report to Congress on the manner of its use. The Attorney General, recognizing this, rightfully provided for an administrative hearing for the exercise of that discretion. On the other hand, he provided by his regulation that his numerous subordinate hearing officers might, in spite of a record clearly establishing a right to relief, deny that relief if, on the basis of undisclosed "confidential" information, the relief would in their opinion be "prejudicial to the public interest, safety, or security." Such a hearing is not an administrative hearing in the American sense of the term. It is no hearing.

Yet, on the basis of such "confidential" information, after more than forty years of residence here, we are tearing petitioner from his relatives and friends and from the country he fought to sustain, when the record shows he has not offended against our laws, bears a good reputation, and would suffer great hardship if deported. Petitioner is not a citizen of the United States, but the Due Process Clause protects "persons." To me, this is not due process. If sanction of this use and effect of "confidential" information is confirmed against this petitioner by a process of judicial reasoning, it may be recognized as a principle of law to be extended against American citizens in a myriad of ways.

I am unwilling to write such a departure from American standards into the judicial or administrative process or to impute to Congress an intention to do so in the absence of much clearer language than it has used here.

Clemente Martinez Perez v. Herbert Brownell, Jr., Attorney General of the United States of America
356 US 44, 2 L ed 2d 603, 78 S Ct 568

Decided March 31, 1958

Clemente Martinez Perez, an American citizen by birth, was declared by the United States District Court for the Northern District of California to have lost his citizenship because he voted in a political election in a foreign country, which, according to the Nationality Act of 1940, is ground for loss of citizenship. This decision was affirmed by the United States Court of Appeals for the Ninth Circuit.

Justice Frankfurter was joined by Justices Burton, Clark, Harlan and Brennan in holding that it was in the power of Congress to enact such provision for loss of citizenship.

Chief Justice Warren, joined by Justices Black and Douglas, dissented on the ground that the government is without *power to take away citizenship from a native-born or lawfully naturalized American. Justice Whittaker also dissented in a separate opinion.*

THE CONGRESS OF THE UNITED STATES has decreed that a citizen of the United States shall lose his citizenship by performing certain designated acts. The petitioner in this case, a native-born American, is declared to have lost his citizenship by voting in a foreign election. Whether this forfeiture of citizenship exceeds the bounds of the Constitution is the issue before us. The problem is fundamental and must be resolved upon fundamental considerations.

Generally, when Congressional action is challenged, constitutional authority is found in the express and implied powers with which the national government has been invested or in those inherent powers that are necessary attributes of a sovereign state. The sweep of those powers is surely broad. In appropriate circumstances, they are adequate to take away life itself. The initial question here is whether citizenship is subject to the exercise of these general powers of government.

What is this government whose power is here being asserted? And what is the source of that power? The answers are the foundation of our Republic. To secure the inalienable rights of the individual, "Governments are instituted among Men, deriving their just powers from the consent of the governed." I do not believe the passage of time has lessened the truth of this proposition. It is basic to our form of government. This government was born of its citizens, it maintains itself in a continuing relationship with them, and, in my judgment, it is without power to sever the relationship that gives rise to its existence. I cannot believe that a government conceived in the spirit of ours was established with power to take from the people their most basic right.

Citizenship is man's basic right, for it is nothing less than the right to have rights. Remove this priceless possession and there remains a stateless person, disgraced and degraded in the eyes of his countrymen. He has no lawful claim to protection from any nation, and no nation may assert rights on his behalf. His very existence is at the sufferance of the state within whose borders he happens to be. In this country the expatriate would presumably enjoy, at most, only the limited rights and privileges of aliens, and like the alien he might even be subject to deportation and thereby deprived of the right to assert any rights. This government was not established with power to decree this fate.

The people who created this government endowed it with broad powers. They created a sovereign state with power to function as a sovereignty. But the citizens themselves are sovereign, and their citizenship is not subject to the general powers of their government. Whatever may be the scope of its powers to regulate the conduct and affairs of all persons within its jurisdiction, a government of the people cannot take away their citizenship simply because one branch of that government can be said to have a conceivably rational basis for wanting to do so.

The basic Constitutional provision crystallizing the right of citizenship is the first sentence of Section 1 of the Fourteenth Amendment. It is there provided that "All persons born or naturalized in the United States, and subject to the jurisdiction thereof, are citizens of the United States and of the State wherein they reside." United States citizenship is thus the Constitutional birthright of every person born in this country. This Court has declared that Congress is without power to alter this effect of birth in the United States.

United States v. Wong Kim Ark, 169 US 649, 703, 42 L ed 890, 910, 18 S Ct 456. The Constitution also provides that citizenship can be bestowed under a "uniform rule of naturalization," but there is no corresponding provision authorizing divestment. Of course, naturalization unlawfully procured can be set aside. But apart from this circumstance, the status of the naturalized citizen is secure. As this Court stated in Osborn v. Bank of United States (US) 9 Wheat 738, 827, 6 L ed 204, 225:

[*The naturalized citizen*] *becomes a member of the society, possessing all the rights of a native citizen, and standing, in the view of the constitution, on the footing of a native. The constitution does not authorize Congress to enlarge or abridge those rights. The simple power of the national Legislature, is to prescribe a uniform rule of naturalization, and the exercise of this power exhausts it, so far as respects the individual.* [*Emphasis added.*]

Under our form of government, as established by the Constitution, the citizenship of the lawfully naturalized and the native-born cannot be taken from them.

There is no question that citizenship may be voluntarily relinquished. The right of voluntary expatriation was recognized by Congress in 1868. Congress declared that "the right of expatriation is a natural and inherent right of all people. . . ." Although the primary purpose of this declaration was the protection of our naturalized citizens from the claims of their countries of origin, the language was properly regarded as establishing the reciprocal right of American citizens to abjure their allegiance. In the early days of this nation the right of expatriation had been a matter of controversy. The common-law doctrine of perpetual allegiance was evident in the opinions of this Court. And, although impressment of naturalized American seamen of British birth was a cause of the War of 1812, the executive officials of this government were not unwavering in their support of the right of expatriation. Prior to 1868 all efforts to obtain Congressional enactments concerning expatriation failed. The doctrine of perpetual allegiance, however, was so ill suited to the growing nation whose doors were open to immigrants from abroad that it could not last. Nine years before Congress acted Attorney General Black stated the American position in a notable opinion:

Here, in the United States, the thought of giving it [the right of expatriation] up cannot be entertained for a moment. Upon that principle this country was populated. We owe to it our existence as a nation. Ever since our independence we have upheld and maintained it by every form of words and acts. We have constantly promised full and complete protection to all persons who should come here and seek it by renouncing their natural allegiance and transferring their fealty to us. We stand pledged to it in the face of the whole world.

It has long been recognized that citizenship may not only be voluntarily renounced through exercise of the right of expatriation but also by other actions in derogation of undivided allegiance to this country. While the essential qualities of the citizen-state relationship under our Constitution preclude the exercise of governmental power to divest United States citizenship, the establishment of that relationship did not impair the principle that conduct of a citizen showing a voluntary transfer of allegiance is an abandonment of citizenship. Nearly all sovereignties recognize that acquisition of foreign nationality ordinarily shows a renunciation of citizenship. Nor is this the only act by which the citizen may show a voluntary abandonment of his citizenship. Any action by which he manifests allegiance to a foreign state may be so inconsistent with the retention of citizenship as to result in loss of that status. In recognizing the consequence of such action, the government is not taking away United States citizenship to implement its general regulatory powers, for, as previously indicated, in my judgment citizenship is immune from divestment under these powers. Rather, the government is simply giving formal recognition to the inevitable consequence of the citizen's own voluntary surrender of his citizenship.

Twice before, this Court has recognized that certain voluntary conduct results in an impairment of the status of citizenship. In Savorgnan v. United States, 338 US 491, 94 L ed 287, 70 S Ct 292, 15 ALR2d 538, an American citizen had renounced her citizenship and acquired that of a foreign state. This Court affirmed her loss of citizenship, recognizing that "From the beginning, one of the most obvious and effective forms of expatriation has been that of naturalization under the laws of another nation." 338 US, at 498. Mackenzie v. Hare, 239 US 299, 60 L ed 297, 36 S Ct 106, Ann Cas 1916E 645, involved an American woman who had married a British national. That decision sustained an act of Congress which provided that her citizenship was suspended for the duration of her marriage. Since it is sometimes asserted that this case is authority for the broad proposition that Congress can take away United States citizenship, it is necessary to examine precisely what the case involved.

The statute which the Court there sustained did not divest Mrs. Mackenzie of her citizenship. It provided that "any American woman who marries a foreigner shall take the nationality of her husband." "At the termination of the marital relation," the statute continues, "she may *resume* her American citizenship. . . ." (Emphasis added.) Her citizenship was not taken away; it was held in abeyance.

This view of the statute is borne out by its history. The 1907 act was passed after the Department of State had responded to requests from both Houses of Congress for a comprehensive study of our own and foreign nationality laws, together with recommendations for new legislation. One of those recommendations, substantially incorporated in the 1907 act, was as follows:

That an American woman who marries a foreigner shall take during coverture the nationality of her husband; but upon termination of the marital relation by death or absolute divorce she may revert to her American citizenship by registering within one year as an American citizen at the most convenient American consulate or by returning to reside in the United States if she is abroad; or if she is in the United States by continuing to reside therein. [Emphasis added.]

This principle of "reversion of citizenship" was a familiar one in our own law, and the law of foreign states. The statute was merely declarative of the law as it was then understood. Although the opinion in *Mackenzie v. Hare* contains some reference to "termination" of citizenship, the reasoning is consistent with the terms of the statute that was upheld. Thus, the Court speaks of Mrs. Mackenzie's having entered a "condition," 239 US, at 312, not as having surrendered her citizenship. "Therefore," the Court concludes, "as long as the relation lasts it is made tantamount to expatriation." *Ibid.* (Emphasis added.)

A decision sustaining a statute that relies upon the unity of interest in the marital community—a common-law fiction now largely a relic of the past—may itself be outdated. However that may be, the foregoing demonstrates that *Mackenzie v. Hare* should not be understood to sanction a power to divest citizenship. Rather this case, like *Savorgnan*, simply acknowledges that United States citizenship can be abandoned, temporarily or permanently, by conduct showing a voluntary transfer of allegiance to another country.

The background of the Congressional enactment pertinent to this case indicates that Congress was proceeding generally in accordance with this approach. After the initial Congressional designation in 1907 of certain actions that were deemed to be an abandonment of citizenship, it became apparent that further clarification of the problem was necessary. In 1933 President Roosevelt, acting at the request of the House Committee on Immigration and Naturalization, established a committee of cabinet members to prepare a codification and revision of the nationality laws. The committee, composed of the Secretary of State, the Attorney General and the Secretary of Labor, spent five years preparing the codification that became the Nationality Act of 1940 and submitted their draft in 1938. It is evident that this committee did not believe citizenship could be divested under the government's general regulatory powers. Rather, it adopted the position that the citizen abandons his status by compromising his allegiance. In its letter submitting the proposed codification to the President, the committee described the loss of nationality provisions in these words:

"They are merely intended to deprive persons of American nationality when such persons, *by their own acts, or inaction, show that their real attachment is to the foreign country and not to the United States*." (Emphasis added.)

Furthermore, when the draft code was first discussed by the House Committee on Immigration and Naturalization —the only legislative group that subjected the codification to detailed examination—it was at once recognized that the status of citizenship was protected from Congressional control by the Fourteenth Amendment. In considering the sit-

uation of a native-born child of alien parentage, Congressmen Poage and Rees, members of the Committee, and
Richard Flournoy, the State Department representative, engaged in the following colloquy:

MR. POAGE. *Isn't that based on the constitutional provision
that all persons born in the United States are citizens
thereof?*

MR. FLOURNOY. *Yes.*

MR. POAGE. *In other words, it is not a matter we have any
control over.*

MR. FLOURNOY. *No; and no one wants to change that.*

MR. POAGE. *No one wants to change that, of course.*

MR. FLOURNOY. *We have control over citizens born abroad,
and we also have control over the question of expatriation.
We can provide for expatriation. No one proposes to
change the constitutional provisions.*

MR. REES. *We cannot change the citizenship of a man who
went abroad, who was born in the United States.*

MR. FLOURNOY. *You can make certain acts of his result in a
loss of citizenship.*

MR. REES. *Surely, that way.*

It is thus clear that the purpose governing the formulation of most of the loss of nationality provisions of the
codification was the specification of acts that would of
themselves show a voluntary abandonment of citizenship.
Congress did not assume it was empowered to use denationalization as a weapon to aid in the exercise of its general
powers. Nor should we.

Section 401 (e) of the 1940 Act added a new category of
conduct that would result in loss of citizenship: "Voting in
a political election in a foreign state or participating in an
election or plebiscite to determine the sovereignty over foreign territory . . ."

The conduct described was specifically represented by Mr. Flournoy to the House Committee as indicative of "a choice of the foreign nationality," just like "using a passport of a foreign state as a national thereof."

The precise issue posed by Section 401(e) is whether the conduct it describes invariably involves a dilution of undivided allegiance sufficient to show a voluntary abandonment of citizenship. Doubtless under some circumstances a vote in a foreign election would have this effect. For example, abandonment of citizenship might result if the person desiring to vote had to become a foreign national or represent himself to be one. Conduct of this sort is apparently what Mr. Flournoy had in mind when he discussed with the Committee the situation of an American-born youth who had acquired Canadian citizenship through the naturalization of his parents. Mr. Flournoy suggested that the young man might manifest an election of nationality by taking advantage of his Canadian citizenship and voting "as a Canadian." And even the situation that bothered Committee Chairman Dickstein—Americans voting in the Saar plebiscite—might under some circumstances disclose conduct tantamount to dividing allegiance. Congressman Dickstein expressed his concern as follows:

"I know we had a lot of Nazis, so-called American citizens, go to Europe who have voted in the Saar for the annexation of territory to Germany, and Germany says that they have the right to participate and to vote, and yet they are American citizens."

There might well be circumstances where an American shown to have voted at the behest of a foreign government to advance its territorial interests would compromise his native allegiance.

The fatal defect in the statute before us is that its application is not limited to those situations that may rationally be said to constitute an abandonment of citizenship. In specifying that any act of voting in a foreign political election results in loss of citizenship, Congress has employed a classification so broad that it encompasses conduct that fails to show a voluntary abandonment of American citizenship. "The connection between the fact proved and that presumed is not sufficient." Manley v. Georgia, 279 US 1, 7, 73 L ed 575, 578, 49 S Ct 215; see also Tot v. United States, 319 US 463, 87 L ed 1519, 63 S Ct 1241; Bailey v. Alabama, 219 US 219, 55 L ed 191, 31 S Ct 145. The reach of this statute is best indicated by a decision of a former Attorney General, holding that an American citizen lost her citizenship under Section 401(e) by voting in an election in a Canadian town on the issue of whether beer and wine should be sold. Voting in a foreign election may be a most equivocal act, giving rise to no implication that allegiance has been compromised. Nothing could demonstrate this better than the political history of this country. It was not until 1928 that a Presidential election was held in this country in which no alien was eligible to vote. Earlier in our history at least twenty-two states had extended the franchise to aliens. It cannot be seriously contended that this nation understood the vote of each alien who previously took advantage of this privilege to be an act of allegiance to this country, jeopardizing the alien's native citizenship. How then can we attach such significance to any vote of a United States citizen in a foreign election? It is also significant that of eighty-four nations whose nationality laws have been compiled by the United Nations, only this country specifically designates foreign voting as an expatriating act.

My conclusions are as follows. The government is without power to take citizenship away from a native-born or lawfully naturalized American. The Fourteenth Amendment recognizes that this priceless right is immune from the exercise of governmental powers. If the government determines that certain conduct by United States citizens should be prohibited because of anticipated injurious consequences to the conduct of foreign affairs or to some other legitimate governmental interest, it may within the limits of the Constitution proscribe such activity and assess appropriate punishment. But every exercise of governmental power must find its source in the Constitution. The power to denationalize is not within the letter or the spirit of the powers with which our government was endowed. The citizen may elect to renounce his citizenship, and under some circumstances he may be found to have abandoned his status by voluntarily performing acts that compromise his undivided allegiance to his country. The mere act of voting in a foreign election, however, without regard to the circumstances attending the participation, is not sufficient to show a voluntary abandonment of citizenship. The record in this case does not disclose any of the circumstances under which this petitioner voted. We know only the bare fact that he cast a ballot. The basic right of American citizenship has been too dearly won to be so lightly lost.

I fully recognize that only the most compelling considerations should lead to the invalidation of Congressional action, and where legislative judgments are involved this Court should not intervene. But the Court also has its duties, none of which demands more diligent performance than that of protecting the fundamental rights of individuals. That duty is imperative when the citizenship of an American is at stake—that status that alone assures him the full enjoyment of the precious rights conferred by our Constitution. As I see my duty in this case, I must dissent.

IV

The Law and the Future

The Chief Justice
Looks Ahead

The Law and the Future

An Article by Chief Justice Warren
Published in the November 1955 Issue
of Fortune Magazine

WHEN A MAN of law tries to peer through the next twenty-five years, he is struck by the probability that all legal systems, and indeed the very concept of law, will be as severely tested as ever in history. The test comes from two sides.

First, the accelerating rate of scientific and technological change in the world makes the pace of legal change look like a tortoise racing a hare. In this same *Fortune* series for which I am writing, it has been predicted by men of science that world-wide transportation may soon become almost as rapid as communication is now; that nuclear developments can make energy almost as cheap as air; that climate control will enable us to turn the Arctic into a tropical garden or alternatively to bring on another Ice Age, as we please. These and like marvels, if achieved, will obviously revolutionize those relationships between man and man, and between man and government, which are the subject matter of the law.

The other test of law comes from the world political situation. The struggle between Communism and freedom, whether hot, cold, or lukewarm, extends not only along the physical frontiers of our civilization, but into its mind and soul, inevitably straining the fabric of all our institutions, the law included. Our legal system is woven around the freedom and dignity of the individual. A Communist state ignores these values. Ours is the difficult task of defending and strengthening these values while also pursuing a goal that sometimes appears to be in conflict with them—namely, the physical security of our nation.

Such are two formidable challenges to the law which seem to line the corridor of the next twenty-five years.

WHY THE CHALLENGES MUST BE MET

Yet no man who understands the nature and purpose of law will let these challenges go by default. There are at least three reasons why an American jurist must work, hope and pray that the observance of law, the prestige of law and the knowledge of law will be far more widespread a generation hence than they are now. I shall give these reasons and then proceed to suggest, as specifically as possible, how I think that hope can be fulfilled.

First of all, the United States, as Americans have always known and loved it, cannot subsist without law. Our Constitution was designed chiefly by lawyers; it was given bone and sinew by great jurists like John Marshall; and we owe the continuity of our social existence to the respect for law of which our reverence for the Constitution is the symbol and sign. Cicero defined a commonwealth as "an agreement of law and a community of interest." Without their agreement of law, Americans might still have some community of interest, but it would unquestionably take one of those barbaric forms in which order is kept by force alone, and in which the freedom of the individual and the consent of the governed is ignored.

In the second place, it is not just the United States that needs law, it is the entire world. The world's chief need in these next decades will be peace and order; and of all human institutions, law has the best historical claim to satisfy this need. Isaiah said that peace is the work of justice. It was an English axiom, framed by Coke, that certainty is the mother of quiet. Justice and certainty are twin aims of the law. When the United States entered the late World War, British soldiers sent the following message to our soldiers: "We welcome you as brothers in the struggle to make sure that the world shall be ruled by the force of law, and not by the law of force." Until the millennium, when all men shall be ruled by Christian love, no other means of social peace but these two—the law of force or the force of law—are likely to be known to man.

The third reason the great mid-century challenges to the law must be met is simply this: the nature of man. In all times and places he has had a sense of justice and a desire for justice. Any child expresses this fact of nature with his first judgment that this or that "isn't fair." A legal system is simply a mature and sophisticated attempt, never perfected but always capable of improvement, to institutionalize this sense of justice and to free men from the terror and unpredictability of arbitrary force. Unfortunately, the same human nature that craves justice and freedom under law is too often willing to deny them to others. Thus the struggle for law is never-ending, and our generation is inevitably engaged in it.

The Supreme Court Building in Washington is adorned with many statues and friezes. Among the figures represented are Menes, Hammurabi, Moses, Solomon, Lycurgus, Solon, Draco, Confucius and Octavian, all lawgivers to people who needed and wanted law before the time of Christ; also Justinian, Mohammed, Charlemagne, King John, St. Louis, Grotius, Blackstone, Napoleon and Marshall, lawgivers since the time of Christ. The history of law is as old as human nature. By the same token, its proper scope is the world. In fact there is no tribe on the face of the earth, however primitive, and no nation, however tyrannical, that is without some customary or formal code of crime and punishment. The problem of law in the next twenty-five years, therefore, is not as much to introduce law anywhere as it is to improve, strengthen and civilize law everywhere. Especially must we broaden the scope of that youngest and most fragile of great legal systems, the law of nations.

What is the American share of this great task? To understand that, we must first understand our own legal system, its strengths and weaknesses.

THE INHERITANCE WE BUILD ON

We Americans are peculiarly fortunate in our legal inheritance. One ancestor of our system is Roman law, of which the legal historian Maine said that it had "the longest known history of any set of human institutions," during which history it was "progressively modified for the better." The nearer ancestor of our system is English law, which has for centuries kept peace throughout an empire and commonwealth wider and more complex than the Roman. Our American modification of these systems has served us equally well. With all its imperfections, it can be called an outstanding success. Of the many characteristics of our legal system that can be given credit for this success, three seem to me especially significant.

First, our legal system has been an organic growth, and not the overnight creation of any individual genius. The founding fathers wrote our Constitution in a single summer, but in doing so they borrowed unashamedly from long-dead lawmakers and political philosophers from Moses and Aristotle to Locke and Montesquieu. In fact they created no novel or untested principles, but chose the best of those already known; and that is one reason their work has endured. The idea of due process, for example, they owed to Magna Charta; the idea of habeas corpus came to them from sources lost in the mists of the Middle Ages. The natural rights of man explicitly asserted by our founding fathers had long been the common-law rights of Englishmen.

Moreover, having written our Constitution, the founding fathers did not use it to abolish and replace the laws to which Americans had been accustomed. The new national system was organically grafted onto the state legal systems, not only those of English, but also those of Latin origin, and has grown along with them to this day. I have already mentioned some of the alien lawgivers whose figures appropriately adorn our Supreme Court Building, and others could be mentioned—Capito and Labeo, Sabinus and Proclus, Gaius and Ulpian—whose very names are known only to scholars of the law, but who made their contributions to its coral-like growth. And the gallery of American law is not complete without representatives of our own colonial, frontier, and state legal experience: eloquent lawyers like Andrew Hamilton, who defended John Peter Zenger and the freedom of the press; brave judges like William Cushing, who advanced alone against the bayonets of Shays' Rebellion and opened the Massachusetts Court; clear thinkers like Chancellor Kent, whose opinions were carried by the authority of reason far beyond the borders of New York. An organic system like ours requires the faithful work of many men, both famous and unknown.

A second reason for the success of our legal system is its adaptability to changing circumstances. As Pollock said, all courts have a duty, which ours generally try to perform, "to keep the rules of law in harmony with the enlightened common sense of the nation." Even the bicycle forced new definitions of negligence in civil suits; and the thousands of other changes forced by later technological developments indicate that our law can keep up with the still greater changes ahead—so long as "the common sense of the nation" can be discerned. Our judges are not monks or scientists, but participants in the living stream of our national life, steering the law between the dangers of rigidity on the one hand and of formlessness on the other. Legal scholars may still debate whether the life of the law is reason, as Coke maintained, or experience, as Holmes claimed. I think it is both. Our system faces no theoretical dilemma but a single continuous problem: how to apply to ever changing conditions the never changing principles of freedom.

So far as the Constitution is concerned, it has demonstrated again and again its capacity for adaptation to the most challenging new conditions. Under John Marshall's leadership, it proved it could mold a strong national government, at a time when such a government was needed to protect American liberties. Later the Constitution had to find a path for those same liberties through the iron mazes of our industrial revolution. And while this quest continues through new electronic mazes, still another challenge confronts the Constitution: Must a nation that is now the strongest in the world demand, for its own further strength and security, a sacrifice by its own citizens of their ancient liberties? This problem haunts the work of all our courts these days. But the Constitution exists for the individual as well as for the nation. I believe it will prove itself adaptable to this new challenge.

There is a third reason for the success of our legal system: While adaptable to our changing national needs, it serves a greater and unchanging cause. That cause is human justice. Ever since Hammurabi published his code to "hold back the strong from oppressing the weak," the success of any legal system is measured by its fidelity to the universal ideal of justice. Theorists beset us with other definitions of law: that it is a mask of privilege, or the judge's private prejudice, or the will of the stronger. But the ideal of justice survives all such myopic views, for as Cicero said, "we are born to it."

The American legal system was nurtured in this ideal of justice and could not last without it. We have in fact accepted not only the rule of law but, through our unique practice of judicial review of legislation, the reign of law. We have done so in the full knowledge that judges are fallible, procedures slow, and the Constitution itself a product of compromise; but in the faith that it is better to make our final decisions in the name of an eternal ideal. Our courts have occasionally misused their great power of review, but never to the point of justifying its forfeiture. They are kept in line with the other branches of government not only by the words of the Constitution, but by a tradition of self-restraint and impersonality.

LAW AND THE GREAT TRADITION

The American constitutional system is in the great tradition which places the fundamental law above the will of the government. This tradition began with the dawn of our civilization. The people of Israel governed themselves as a federation of tribes, without any central government, under a constitution—the Covenant they had made with Jehovah. Even after they chose a king ("that we also may be like all the nations") they kept the tradition because the King, too, lived and ruled under the Covenant. When Rome was young, many a similar commonwealth and republic flourished around the Mediterranean; but Rome survived them all because it employed and extended the rule of law, thus making its greatest contribution to our civilization. When the Renaissance broke the mold of medieval Europe, England was not the only monarchy that gave promise of constitutional development. But England alone avoided a serious relapse into despotism, because England secured its public order and individual freedom under the law.

The sign of this great tradition, the tradition which places the fundamental law above the will of the government, is an independent judiciary. We associate it with our system of separated powers and judicial review; but other nations have maintained the tradition with other forms of government. Britain's system of parliamentary supremacy, for example, can override but does not overawe British justice.

Why, then, have some nations maintained and strengthened the great tradition and not others? For one reason only, that the people were determined to remain free and to keep the law above the government. When the Hitler occupation tried to bend the Supreme Court of Norway to its will, the entire Court risked death by resigning. This act, I am sure, did as much to preserve independent justice for Norway as did *Marbury v. Madison* for the United States, or as Coke's defiance of his dictatorial King did for England. No form of Government, however nearly perfect, can itself secure justice and freedom under law for any country. The true safeguard is the spirit and devotion of the people, a passion for justice and freedom that is widely shared and deeply felt.

To summarize: Americans have one of the great legal systems, but not a monopoly of the sense of justice, which is universal; nor have we a permanent copyright on the means of securing justice, for it is the spirit and not the form of law that keeps justice alive. But as a nation directly challenged by the march of a revolutionary technology, and also by a reactionary antagonist representing the law of force, we have a vital interest in defending and extending the rule of law throughout the world. How then can we go about it?

NEEDED REFORMS OF OUR SYSTEM

Two generations ago Dean Ames of the Harvard Law School pointed out that "the spirit of reform which during the last six hundred years has been bringing our system of law more and more into harmony with moral principles has not yet achieved its perfect work"; and he urged that past advances should encourage effort for future improvement. This advice still needs to be heeded. The proud inscription on our Federal courts—"Equal Justice under Law"—remains our goal but is not fully secured to all our citizens. The rights promised them by our Constitution are not yet perfected.

Some of the defects in our system are inherited; others keep creeping in. Justice, like freedom, needs constant vigilance. Justice delayed is often justice denied. This kind of denial is a growing problem in our Federal courts. Some calendars are so crowded that litigants cannot be sure of trial within four years or more. To our Judicial Conference (composed of the Chief Justice and the Chief Judges of the circuit courts) this has been a problem of increasing concern. It will require a combined effort by the bench, the bar and the litigating public, as well as some help from Congress, to clear this growing backlog and keep the channels of justice open.

Unequal justice is a contradiction in terms. Yet access to justice is unequal in parts of our country. Suspects are sometimes arrested, tried and convicted without being adequately informed of their right to counsel. Even when he knows of this right, many a citizen cannot afford to exercise it. There are barely half enough public defenders, legal-aid societies or other methods available to perfect this right.

American law is pockmarked with other procedural flaws and anachronisms. We have recently made some progress in simplifying methods of appeal in the Federal courts, but much remains to be done. Thanks to outside underwriting, our entire system of administering criminal justice is undergoing a detailed survey by the American Bar Foundation. The facts already known warrant a continuing crusade by the legal profession for fairer and speedier procedures.

Lawyers are officers of the court and therefore servants of justice. Now that the more cynical forms of "legal realism" are growing less fashionable, it is to be hoped that fewer lawyers will regard their professional training as a mere means of livelihood. But cynicism and apathy are not confined to our profession. Since the instinct of justice is universal, every citizen, lawyer or not, can serve justice by living more consciously in its spirit, and by keeping his own vigilant watch on the rights he shares with his fellow citizen. Solon, asked how justice could be secured in Athens, replied, "If those who are not injured feel as indignant as those who are."

WHOSE BILL OF RIGHTS?

This is especially good advice at a time when our Bill of Rights is under subtle and pervasive attack, as at present. The attack comes not only from without, but from our own indifference and failure of imagination. Minorities whose rights are threatened are quicker to band together in their own defense than in the defense of other minorities. The same is true, with less reason, of segments of the majority. Churchmen are quick to defend religious freedom; lawyers were never so universally aroused as by President Roosevelt's Court bill; newspapers are most alert to civil liberties when there is a hint of press censorship in the air. And educators become perturbed at every attempt to curb academic freedom. But too seldom do all of these become militant when ostensibly the rights of only one group are threatened. They do not always react to the truism that when the rights of any individual or group are chipped away, the freedom of all erodes.

The moral is that if each minority, each professional group, and each citizen would imagine himself in the other's shoes, everybody's rights would have firmer support. The beginning of justice is the capacity to generalize and make objective one's private sense of wrong, thus turning it to public account. The pursuit of justice is not the vain pursuit of a remote abstraction; it is a continuing direction for our daily conduct.

Thus it is that when the generation of 1980 receives from us the Bill of Rights, the document will not have exactly the same meaning it had when we received it from our fathers. We will pass on a better Bill of Rights or a worse one, tarnished by neglect or burnished by growing use. If these rights are real, they need constant and imaginative application to new situations. For example: the security procedures set up to protect the Federal Government have been extended to the point where more than eight million Americans must undergo them. As the system expands, everyone is more closely affected by the balance we strike between security and freedom. Injustices carry a wider import. The Bill of Rights must be measured daily against this new problem.

NO UNITED STATES MONOPOLY

By thus improving the administration of justice and strengthening liberty under law in our own country, we will make our greatest single contribution to the promotion of law elsewhere in the world. For as long as the United States leads the forces of freedom in the world's great ideological struggle, our institutions will remain under a global spotlight, and what we do will speak much louder than what we say. If our actions continuously testify to our belief in justice, other free nations will be fortified in their pursuit of the same ideal.

A vital concern for the ideal of justice is what all legal systems most need today. The variety of legal systems need not trouble us; they are like different languages. Some languages are subtler or richer, some more logical or straightforward than others; but all serve the common purpose of communication. So all good legal systems, with their varying histories and environments, serve justice as their people see it; and the best of them serve the great tradition of government under law. But as languages can enrich and extend communication by translations and borrowings, so too can legal systems. The promotion of law in the world will therefore benefit from a revival of comparative jurisprudence, a revival in which American lawyers are already taking an active part.

Twice in our history, in 1883 and 1915, the Lord Chief Justice of England has sat by invitation as an observer on the bench of the United States Supreme Court. I was accorded a similar courtesy last summer in Norway, where I heard proceedings before their Supreme Court; and I also met with the members of Germany's constitutional court in their conference room. At Salzburg, I visited the seminar where American institutions, including American law, are interpreted to deeply interested students from all parts of free Europe; Chief Judge Magruder of our First Circuit Court of Appeals was a lecturer this year. Leading law schools both here and in Europe are giving increased attention to comparative law.

It seems clear that this mutual interest and curiosity can profitably be carried much further. Moslem lands, for example, have old and well-developed legal systems about which American jurists know very little, as do Moslems about ours. An agreement among different cultures to exchange full information on basic points of comparative law—such as why, and under what conditions, a man may be jailed—should lead to considerable self-examination and improvement on all sides. In investigating why a thief may have his hand cut off in Saudi Arabia, or be branded on the forehead in other countries, we might also be led to study some debatable forms of punishment still used in some of our states. Habeas corpus, a right we regard as fundamental to a free society, is not so regarded in some other democracies; why not? Why are British court procedures so much more orderly and rapid than ours? To pursue such inquiries in a spirit of mutual truth-seeking could surely yield good results. All of us have much to teach and much to learn.

WORLD LAW AND THE UN

The United Nations exists because civilized nations prefer orderly, rational and peaceful procedures in the settlement of disputes. This preference is the cradle of law. The UN can become the growing point of a true international legal system, but only as it grows around the ideal of justice. The UN must therefore bend its efforts to make justice the keystone of its arch.

Three ways to do this suggest themselves. First, as justice is a universal goal, so should the membership of the UN transcend its origin as a league of wartime allies, and become as nearly universal as an acceptance of the charter obligations permits. Second, peaceful procedures imply that agreements will be inviolable. There will be great need for the strict honoring of UN agreements in the next twenty-five years, and the nations with the best record in this respect will have done the most to advance the cause of justice under law. Third, more and more international questions can become justiciable, giving a steadily wider jurisdiction to the World Court.

The UN has inevitably been an arena of power politics and ideological struggle. This need not discourage those who hope to see it develop into a focus of world law. It was during one of history's earlier great struggles, the Thirty Years War, that Hugo Grotius of Holland brought to birth those concepts of international law that were to moderate international behavior for three centuries. The UN has not succeeded in writing a generally satisfactory Bill of Human Rights. This does not mean that there is no measure of international agreement on this vital subject. Last June an International Congress of Jurists, composed of lawyers, judges and teachers from forty-nine nations, showed an astonishing unanimity in their so-called Act of Athens, defining the basic characteristics of a free system. They declared that the state is subject to the law and owes its citizens the means to enforce their rights; that judges should uphold the rule of law in entire political independence; that lawyers of the world should insist on a fair trial for every accused; and that the rights of the individual, to be protected by the rule of law include freedom of speech, press, worship, assembly, association and free elections. If by 1980 this writ should run through all the nations whose lawyers helped frame it, then indeed will the great tradition of government under law be established beyond challenge in our world.

Whether or not law can tame the ideological struggles of this era, there is another broad field of human intercourse which can and should be brought wholly within orderly procedures. This is the economic field, where rivalries have sometimes bred wars in the past but need not again. Governments have spent millions of man-hours, as well as billions of dollars, on world economic problems since World War II. They have not solved these problems, but they are learning to manage them. New types of treaties and commissions have proliferated throughout the field of international trade, investment and finance. Within the free world, if we have the will, these orderly procedures and expert institutions can be made to temper all economic controversies and prevent them from becoming inflammatory. We can reasonably resolve that this whole field will be subordinated to peaceful procedures during the next twenty-five years. Justice in the economic sphere often consists in finding a genuine mutuality of interest. Among the free nations, that mutuality is already great, and can be made permanent.

THE HERITAGE AND THE STRUGGLE

Such are the chief growing points from which the law may extend its influence over the affairs of men in the next generation. In doing so it faces the challenge (already mentioned) of an accelerating technology and a world political struggle for survival.

The challenge of technology to the law is largely to its rate of change. To meet it, the law need not itself get more technically complex than it is now; rather the opposite may be its best course. For in self-defense against a technology which only a few can hope to master, the average man and the common sense of justice will seek an ally in laws which all can understand. As in Blackstone's time, some knowledge of law may become "an essential part of a liberal education"; and lawyers, reaffirming their purpose in life to serve justice, may come in closer touch with the deepest springs of our democracy.

The world political struggle is more dangerous to the future of law. It is a struggle of greater proportions than Americans have known before. In some of our wars, we have briefly succumbed to the temptation of imitating the vices of our antagonist; but the national sense of justice and respect for law always returned with peace. In the present struggle between our world and Communism, the temptation to imitate totalitarian security methods is a subtle temptation that must be resisted day by day, for it will be with us as long as totalitarianism itself. The whole question of man's relation to his nation, his government, his fellow man is raised in acute and chronic form. Each of the 462 words of our Bill of Rights, the most precious part of our legal heritage, will be tested and retested.

By 1980 that heritage can be stronger and brighter than ever, and the ideal of liberty and justice under law made more real in its various forms throughout the world. But it will require a new dedication and a continuing faith from all who cherish the heritage and the goal.